Enterprisewide Resource Planning

Enterprisewide Resource Planning
Theory and Practice

Rahul V. Altekar

Senior Functional Architect, JDA India
Hyderabad
and
Visiting Faculty: NITIE, Prin. Welingkars, and XIM, Mumbai

PHI Learning Private Limited

New Delhi-110001

2011

Rs. 150.00

ENTERPRISEWIDE RESOURCE PLANNING: Theory and Practice
Rahul V. Altekar

ISBN-978-81-203-2633-0

The export rights of this book are vested solely with the publisher.

Seventh Printing ... ... September, 2011

Published by Asoke K. Ghosh, PHI Learning Private Limited, M-97, Connaught Circus, New Delhi-110001 and Printed by Mudrak, 30-A, Patparganj, Delhi-110091.

To

My Son Prachetas

Contents

Preface

In one of the corporate training programmes, I had come across a person who motivated me to write this book. He was the *key user* of an ERP system in one of the biggest Indian companies and was totally frustrated to the extent that he had developed certain 'aversion' against ERP and especially against ERP consultants. Even though I felt somewhat emotionally exhausted after interacting with him for long sessions, discussions with him motivated me to share the *complete theory of ERP* with ERP users as well as with the students of ERP. Then it took over three years to the development of this textbook from initial concepts. The book is primarily aimed at providing a stable foundation of knowledge for entry-level students through senior-level practitioners.

The common understanding of ERP system today is that it is a large computer system that integrates all business application programs required by various functional entities, but the underlying principles and disciplines of ERP are not very clear to most of the ERP users and even to ERP consultants. Hence we find certain amount of dissatisfaction and underutilization of ERP systems in India. The fundamental idea that the ERP software such as SAP or Baan is not ERP but a *tool for ERP* is not yet understood by Indian companies. Unfortunately, we do not find a comprehensive literature that explains the ERP concepts with its associated theory, and the practical implementation guidelines with cases, especially in the Indian context. Keeping these requirements in mind, the presentation of the book is planned to provide the organized approaches to (ERP related) problem solving by highlighting the different ways to ERP adoption, not based on the whims of individual ERP software developers but on the cultural aspects coupled with the **best practices.**

The book is divided into two parts. In Part I the overall theory of ERP is discussed, whereas Part II focuses on current ERP scenario in India and its possible optimization.

Part I contains six chapters on ERP theory with a number of flowcharts, screenshots and figures. Chapter 1 introduces the reader to ERP and its general features. Chapter 2 highlights the conceptual model of ERP and its evolution over a period of time and also defines the basic architecture of ERP. Attempts are made here to make the reader grasp the complete necessities of ERP system. Chapter 3 details the important world-class practices and their practical implications.

Further, it provides a generalized understanding of the core logic of ERP culture. Chapter 4 introduces the current ERP market scenario and strategies played by ERP vendors, especially in the Indian context. It explains the strengths of various ERP brands and how critical their selection procedure is. Chapter 5 provides the basic functionalities offered by any ERP software. It discusses at length various major modules like Manufacturing, Distribution and Financial, and submodules including Item Control, Formula Management, MPS Control, MRP Control, CRP Control, Purchase Control, Finance Control, etc. These discussions are supported with necessary diagrams, flowcharts and actual screen shots captured from reputed ERP brands. The idea is to help the reader get a feel of ERP functionalities and their strengths. Chapter 6 throws light on the fundamentals of ERP implementation methodology. It points out the importance of BPR in ERP implementation with its elements, costs and steps in execution. Various real-life examples of implementations are explained to make the theme clearer.

Part II contains two chapters focusing on the practical side of ERP in India. Chapter 7 contains current "As Is" status of ERP in the Indian corporate sector. It has been emphasized that the chief issue of ERP is neither the process nor the technology but the people. The core strength of ERP consulting could be the ability to recognize the elemental human characteristics and their impact on ERP systems, especially in Indian companies. To support this view, a number of cases of ERP mishaps are explained with their root causes. To address these issues and to make ERP a success, in Chapter 8, I have conceptualized the **ERP *Panchaga*** (five-element) model to enable the consultants, project managers, key-users, or even students of ERP subjects to anticipate and resolve the difficulties involved and minimize the negative effects of ERP adoption programme in India.

In sum, it is expected that this book would help readers understand the scope of ERP with its integration abilities, the need for third party consulting support, the overall expenses, and also the crucial role played by end-users. The target readers are management and final-year engineering students. Also, the book is so designed that those ERP professionals who have either experienced the ERP or preparing for it will receive fundamental inputs to strengthen their views and strategies to make ERP a success.

I hope this work will meet its objectives and will contribute significantly to ERP literature.

I take this opportunity to thank all my industry colleagues with whom I had long and fruitful discussions. I also wish to gratefully aknowledge the inputs and the real-life experience I have gained from Indian companies on the many facets and multidimensional aspects of ERP. I sincerely thank everyone who has helped me, directly or indirectly, in the preparation of this text. My special thanks are due to my family members, especially my wife who had put in extra efforts in reviewing many of the ideas presented in the book.

Any constructive comments for improving the contents will be warmly appreciated.

Rahul V. Altekar

PART I
THEORY OF ERP

CHAPTER 1 Introduction

Before the industrial revolution, very few companies were doing the business in an organized way or in a corporate style as is the case today. These companies were small, and in most cases, a single person was managing all the operational and the related functions. The decisions were made keeping in mind the overall company objectives and available resources. Slowly, the market demand and manufacturing scales of the companies grew, and managing the entire operations became impossible for a single person. More and more people were brought in and the different business functions were given to different individuals. Thus, in the larger organization, each senior person was provided with next level people to assist him or her and the various departments evolved. The size of the department began to increase, as more and more people were required to do the job.

As the *department* concept became popular, it was designed to be specific to a *function*. Thus, the Accounts Department was made responsible for all the financial transaction of the management, whereas the Purchase Department was made responsible for procurement of goods and services only. In the process of this evolution, departments became large, specialized, and functionally watertight. Each had its own set of procedures. Employees, at most levels within a department would just collect and pass on the information upward. Thus, information was shared between departments only at the top level. It was also common that the "necessary" information for one department could be "waste" for the other. Such industry environment prevailed for many decades.

The times have changed today from such a highly secured corporate working environment to the more uncertain future. Now the difference between market leaders and followers, or successful companies and other companies is defined as the way companies make use of generated information. In fact, it is said that companies have to manage the future by sustaining today through managing the current and future business information.

Hence we find a trend today to generate huge amount of data – Financial data, customer data, purchase and supplier data, employee data, and so on. The organization that makes best possible use of this information will succeed in retaining the existing market as well as improving the share of the market. That is the exact reason behind the huge investments in computers and software made by all the reputed companies in the world. This phenomenon was started since 1970s and today it has culminated in highly sophisticated IT solutions.

Initially, IT had provided with good results by automating the existing business functions and discrete procedures. Most of this happened by implementing a range of software in various departments, but without its complete integration with the corporate strategy. Some examples of such IT systems are MRP, MRP-II, Finance Management, Integrated Materials Management systems, SCADA based manufacturing systems, etc.

The major problem faced by the users in such systems was effective information collecting, summarizing, and refining huge amount of data, which is a daunting task. People from various departments having different job profiles and objectives alone cannot make use of systems to the fullest extent. In order to manage information in terms of delivering high quality support to the right decision makers at the right time, one must automate the process of data collection, refine the date and give proper information to the organization. To achieve this, one must make information technology an ally and should harness its full potential and use it in the best possible way. This is the exact reason why the Enterprise-wide Resource Planning (ERP) concept originated and almost all organizations are switching to ERP package as a solution.

To draw real benefits from technology, one should have a total view of enterprise. Such a system has to work around the core activities of organizations and should facilitate the flow of information across departmental barriers. This system can thus be called Enterprise Resource Planning System.

WHAT IS ERP CONCEPT?

An *Enterprise* is a group of people with a common goal, having resources to achieve that goal. Resources include money, manpower, materials, machines, technologies, etc. Planning is putting necessary functions in place and putting them together.

Enterprise-wide resource planning (ERP) is a planning philosophy enabled with software that attempts to integrate all the business processes of different departments and functions across a company onto a single computer system that can serve particular needs of the different departments. Typically, before ERP implementation, each department has its own computer system optimized for the requirements that a department needs. As shown in Figure 1.1, each department will maintain separate databases and design applications as per their functionalities. These will result in *local optima* and overall very poor results across all the departments or within the company.

ERP combines all the business requirements of the company together into a single, integrated software program that runs off a single database so that the various departments can more easily share information and communicate with each other. As shown in Figure 1.2, conceptually ERP replaces the old standalone computer systems in finance, HR, manufacturing, etc., with a single software

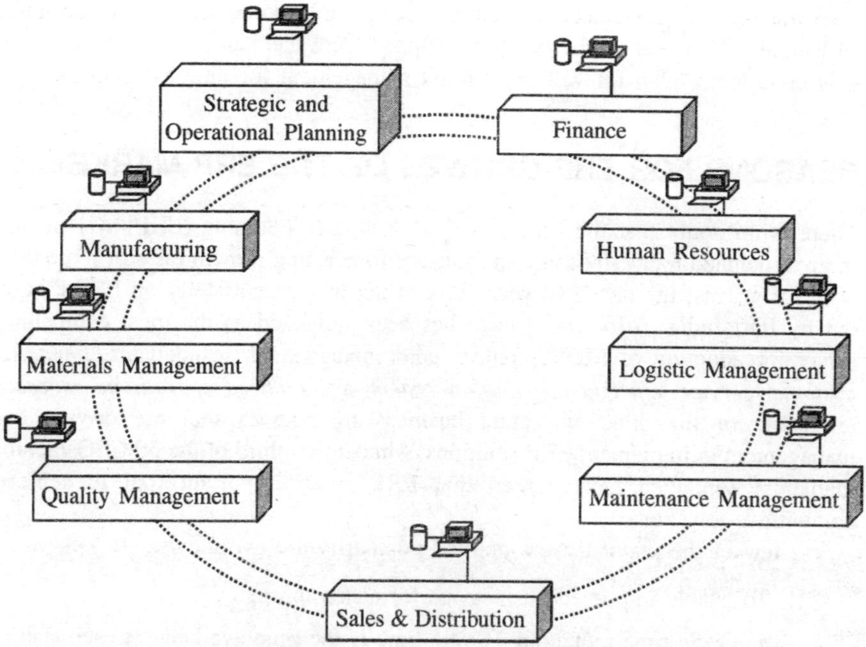

Figure 1.1 Stand alone systems.

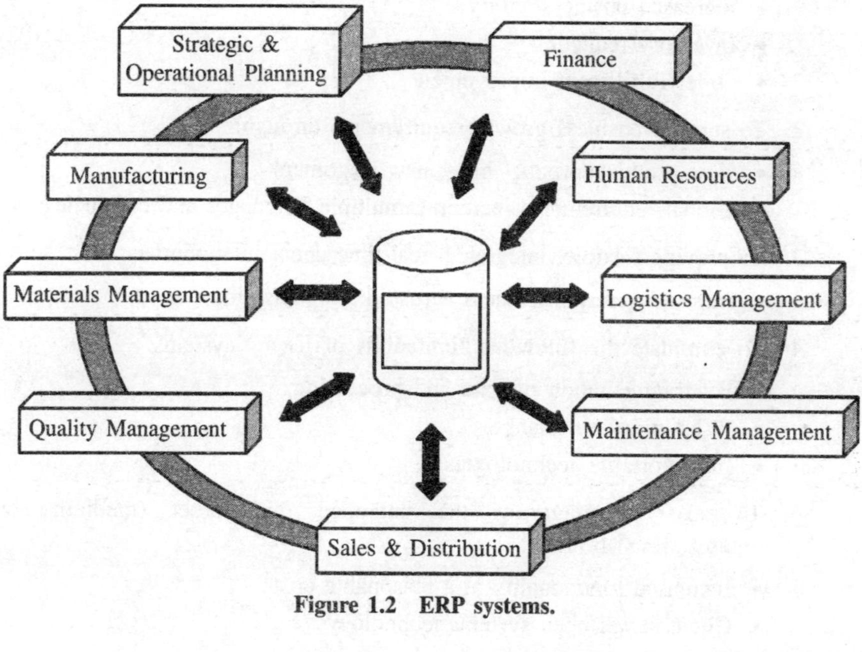

Figure 1.2 ERP systems.

program that facilitates various functional modules. Thus everybody from the finance, manufacturing, purchasing, etc. will still get their own advantages of software, along with the added feature of availability of information across other departments to improve decision quality. For example, someone in finance can use ERP to see if any sale order has been shipped from the warehouse so that he can now confidently plan for working capital management for the next period.

REASONS FOR THE GROWTH OF THE ERP MARKET

There is no doubt that the Enterprisewide Resource Planning (ERP) systems are in great demand today. Industry analysts are forecasting growth rates of more than 30% for at least the next five years. According to a recent study on ERP carried out by IDC India, *corporate growth* has been indicated as the most compelling driver for adoption of ERP amongst senior management respondents. *Improved customer service*, *efficient distribution system*, and *reduced operational expenses* are some of the other important business imperatives that are driving top management to implement ERP solutions. Almost two-third of the 50 CEOs/Senior managers contacted have agreed that ERP is an important tool to achieve competitive advantage.

A few of the major drivers of ERP popularity are as follows:

1. To enable improved business performance through:
   - Cycle time reduction—Cycle time is the time available at each station for the performance of the work allocated or the time elapsing between completed units coming of an assembly line.
   - Increased business agility
   - Inventory reduction
   - Order fulfillment improvement
2. To support business growth requirements through:
   - New products/product lines, new customers
   - Global requirements including multiple languages and currencies
3. To provide flexible, integrated, real-time decision support in:
   - Improving responsiveness across the organization
4. To eliminate the following limitations of legacy systems:
   - By fragmentation of data and processing
   - Inflexibility to change
   - Insupportable technologies
5. To take advantage of the untapped mid-market (medium size organizations) through:
   - Increased functionality at a reasonable cost
   - Client server/open systems technology
   - Vertical market solutions

These are some of the reasons for the explosive growth rate of the ERP markets and the ERP vendors. As more and more companies are entering into the market, the ERP vendors are shifting their focus from big companies to different market segments of medium and small size companies. In future, it may not be easy to capture a good market share and improve on it, and this may lead to a lot of mergers and acquisitions of ERP vendors for gaining strategic and competitive advantages.

EXERCISES

1. Why are ERP packages are becoming popular in Indian market?
2. Explain the role played by IT in traditional organization set-ups.
3. What is the difference between SCADA based automation software and ERP?
4. Enlist at least 10 ERP vendors, who are offering their brands in India.

CHAPTER 2

Origin, Evolution and Structure

We have mentioned some of the reasons that made the ERP concept popular and enabled it to spread across the world. Let us now discuss the complete theory of ERP and its application scenarios.

CONCEPTUAL MODEL OF ERP

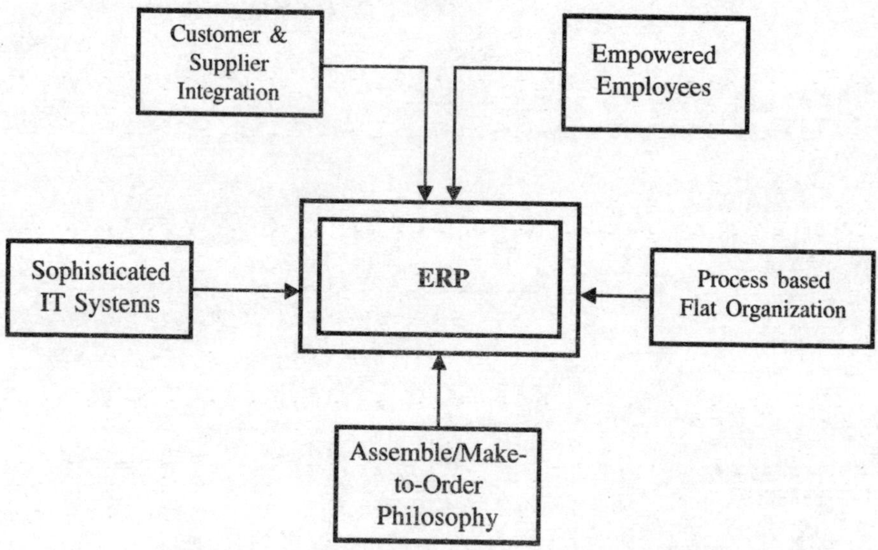

Figure 2.1 Conceptual ERP model: pillars of ERP.

Figure 2.1 shows the conceptual model on which ERP theory is based. We can see that the ERP concept defines the five measures that govern business policies:

1. Process based flat organization
2. Assemble-to-order or Make-to-order philosophy
3. Empowered employees
4. Customer and supplier integration
5. Sophisticated IT systems.

These business policies lead to critical elements for ERP system, and the success of ERP depends on the level of their adoption in the organization. We will deal with these issues later in Chapter 8.

Keeping the above-mentioned concept in minds ERP can be defined in the following ways:

1. It is a planning methodology or philosophy that is based on the seamless integration of all the business processes of an enterprise.
2. It is a set of software covering major business areas e.g. finance, logistics, sales, materials, manufacturing, distribution, all so tightly integrated with one another that any business activity recorded at one place is immediately reflected in all other places.
3. It is the finest expression of the inseparability of Info-tech and business. An enterprise-wide system with enabling technology and effective managerial tool for integrating all the levels and improving reportabilty.

The above definitions explain the fundamental design feature of ERP as **system based business solution.** ERP integrates the various departments and functions throughout the organization. It attempts to assimilate everything into a single system that can serve every department and functional needs. While doing so, it focuses on the business plan areas and addresses those problems with integrated planning approach.

To understand how ERP is a system based business solution, we have to first critically examine the two key words 'System' and 'Solution'.

System: According to Webster's Dictionary (2002), a system is "a combination of elements or parts achieving a unique goal". In the present context, we can say that ERP is a system for a specific set or arrangement of elements which are organized to accomplish a pre-defined goal through processing of information. This goal invariably could be to support existing business function, improve the transparency of data, improve efficiency in business, improve decision making, and provide improved customer (internal as well as external) satisfaction. The key resource elements of such a system are hardware (switches, V-sat, routers, server, etc.), software (languages ABAP, VB), users, databases, etc.

Solution: The dictionary meaning of solution is "an explanation or answer to a problem". But here we are specifically speaking about **business solutions.** A business solution can be interpreted as a framework encompassing strategy, organization structures, key performance indicators, measurements and IT, which must be aligned to the business processes. Conventionally, there are three kinds of business processes—acquiring and paying for input resources, converting inputs into finished goods and services, and selling and collecting payment from customers for the goods and services provided.

Thus, ERP as a combination of system and business solution provides the user with an effective planning tool.

THE EVOLUTION OF ERP

ERP is an outcome of 40 years of trial and error. It has evolved as a strategic tool because of continuous improvement in the available techniques to manage business and the fast growth of information technology. Figure 2.2 shows the various phases of development in relation to time, development in resource planning systems, and the evolution of the concept of ERP.

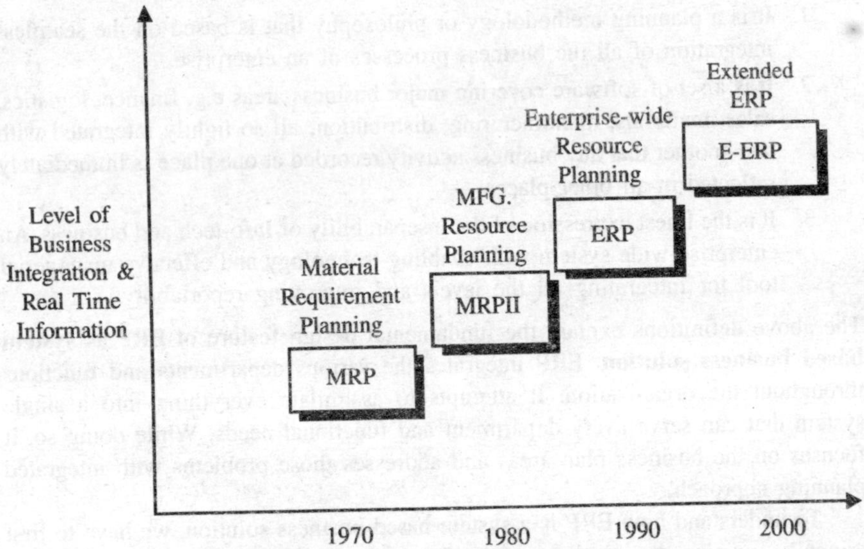

Figure 2.2 ERP: Historical overview.

Prior to 1960s, business had to rely on the traditional ways of inventory management to ensure smooth functioning of the organization. These theories are called *classical inventory management* or *scientific inventory control methods*. The most popularly known amongst them is **EOQ (Economic Order Quantity)**. In this method, each item in the stock is analyzed for its ordering cost and the inventory carrying cost. A trade off is established on a phased out expected demand of one year, and this way the most economic ordering quantity can be decided. This technique in principle is a deterministic way of managing inventory. The formula for EOQ is

$$EOQ = (2DS/IC)$$

where

D = annual demand
S = cost of placing an order
IC = total inventory carrying cost per unit.

Along with EOQ, we find various inventory models such as fixed order quantity, periodic order method, optional replenishment method, etc., which were in practice earlier. These theories were very popular in pre-MRP era.

In 1960s, a new technique of Material Requirements Planning, popularly known as MRP, was evolved. This was a proactive manner of inventory management. This technique fundamentally explodes the end product demand obtained from the *Master Production Schedule (MPS)* for a specified product structure (which is taken from Bill of Material) into a detailed schedule of purchase orders or production orders, taking into account the inventory on hand. MRP is a simple logic but the magnitude of data involved in a realistic situation makes it computationally cumbersome. If undertaken manually, the entire process is highly time consuming. It therefore becomes essential to use a computer to carry out the exercise.

MRP successfully demonstrated its effectiveness in reduction of inventory, production, and delivery lead times by improving coordination and avoiding delays, thus making commitments more realistic. MRP proved to be a very good technique for managing inventory, but it did not take into account other resources of an organization. In 1970s, this gave birth to a modified MRP logic, popularly known as *closed loop MRP*. In this technique, the capacity of the organization to produce a particular product is also taken into account by incorporating a module called **capacity requirements planning (CRP)**. Hence, a feedback loop is provided from the CRP module to MPS if there is not enough capacity available to produce.

In 1980s, the need was felt to integrate the financial resources with the manufacturing activities. From this evolved an integrated manufacturing management system called **Manufacturing Resources Planning (MRP II)**. MRP II was thus included in MRP and CRP, along with necessary financial information. In fact the APICS (American Production and Inventory Control Society) definition explains the exact difference between closed loop MRP and MRP II. It defines MRP II as:

> A method for effective planning of all the resources of manufacturing company. Ideally it addresses operational planning in units, financial planning in dollars and has a simulation capability to answer 'what-if' questions. It is made up of a variety of functions each linked together: Business Planning, Production Planning, Master Production Scheduling, Material Requirements Planning, Capacity Requirements Planning and the execution system for capacity and priority. Outputs from these systems would be integrated with financial reports, such as the business plan, the purchase commitment report, shipping, budget, inventory production, etc.

Transition from MRP-II to ERP happened during 1980 to 1990. The basic MRP II system design was suffering from a few inherent drawbacks such as limited focus to manufacturing activities, assumption of the mass or repetitive production set ups, and poor budgetary and costing controls.

Over the years, new business philosophies evolved, such as customer oriented manufacturing (lean production systems), activity based costing, third party logistics, warehousing, quality systems like ISO-9000, zero inspection, supplier partnership, etc.

The shortcomings of MRP-II and the need to integrate these new techniques, led to the development of a total integrated solution called ERP, which attempts to integrate the transactions of suppliers and customers with the manufacturing and service environment of the organization to produce the best possible plan. Today, we see further development in the ERP concept and evolution of E-ERP (extended ERP or web-enable ERP), which is in turn evolving into SCM (Supply Chain Management) solutions like APS (Advanced Planning and Scheduling).

The complete overview of ERP, indicating its scope and boundaries is shown in Figure 2.3.

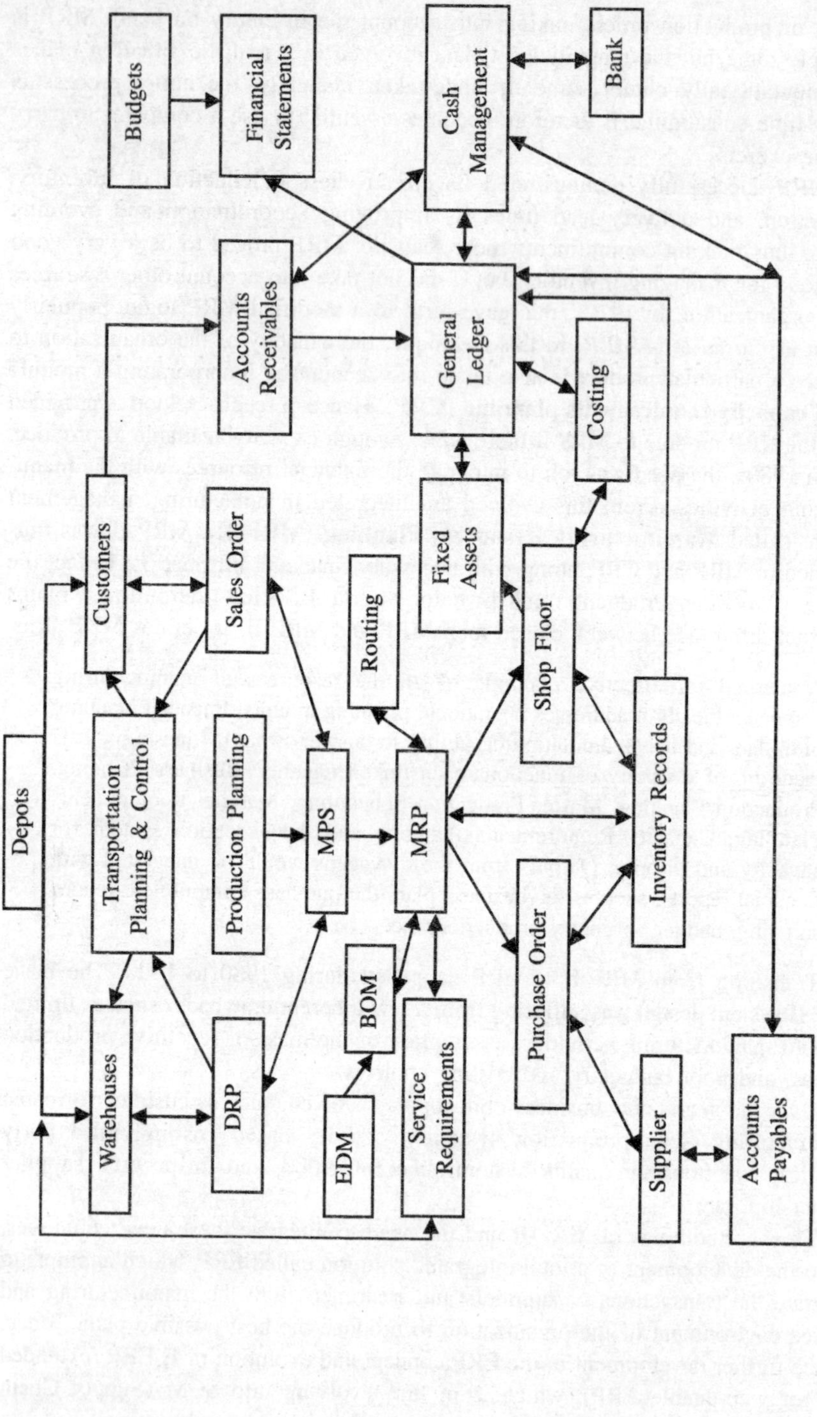

Figure 2.3 Complete overview of ERP.

THE STRUCTURE OF ERP

The essence of ERP is the fundamental approach which takes a holistic view of the subject. The traditional application systems, which the organizations generally employ, treat each transaction separately. They are built around the strong boundaries of specific functions that a specific application is meant to cater. ERP considers them to be the part of the interlinked processes that make up the total business and financial impact. Almost all the typical application systems are nothing but the data manipulation tools. They store data, process them, and present them in the appropriate form whenever requested by the user. In this process, the only problem is that there is no link between the application systems being used by different departments. An ERP system also does the same thing, but in a different manner. There are hundreds of such data tables which store data generated as a result of diverse transactions, but they are not confined to any departmental or functional boundaries. These are rather integrated for the speedy and accurate results required by multiple users, for multiple purposes, for multiple sites, and at multiple times.

Thus ERP solution implies that it be:

- **Flexible:** An ERP system should be flexible to respond to the changing needs of an enterprise. The client server technology enables ERP to run across various database backends through Open Data Base Connectivity (ODBC).
- **Modular:** The ERP system has to have modular application architecture. This means that various functionalities are logically clubbed into different business processes and structured into a module which can be interfaced or detached whenever required without affecting the other modules. It should support multiple hardware platforms for the companies having heterogeneous collection of systems. It must support some third party add-ons also.
- **Comprehensive:** It should be able to support variety of organizational functions and must be suitable for a wide range of business organizations.
- **Beyond the company:** It should not be confined to the organizational boundaries, rather, it should support the on-line connectivity to the other business entities of the organization. This feature is the recent development and such ERP solution is referred to as *E-ERP*, or *extended ERP concept*.
- **Belonging to the best business practices:** It must have a collection of the best business processes applicable worldwide.

To make use of the above advantages, **ERP Architecture** must be designed using the advanced information technologies and environments. Thus, ERP is typically implemented through a client-server environment. This technology divides the applications fundamentally into two or more components, called *Server* and *Client(s)*. The client portion uses the functions of the server. Servers are centralized while clients tend to be spread out in multiple locations.

The popular types of ERP architecture are two-tier architecture and three-tier architecture. These are now explained in detail.

Two-tier Architecture

In this type, the server handles application and database duties. The clients present the data and pass user input back to the server. While there may be multiple servers and the clients may be distributed across several types of local and wide area links, this distribution of processing responsibilities remains the same. Figure 2.4 depicts the two-tier architecture.

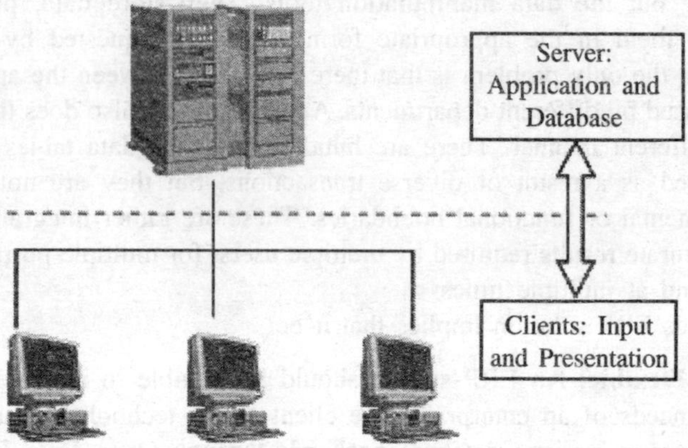

Figure 2.4 Two-tier architecture.

Three-tier Architecture

In three-tier architectures, the database and application functions are separated. In this scenario, satisfying client requests requires two or more network connections. Initially, the client establishes communications with the application server. The application server then creates a second connection to the database server. Figure 2.5 gives a pictorial view of three-tier architecture.

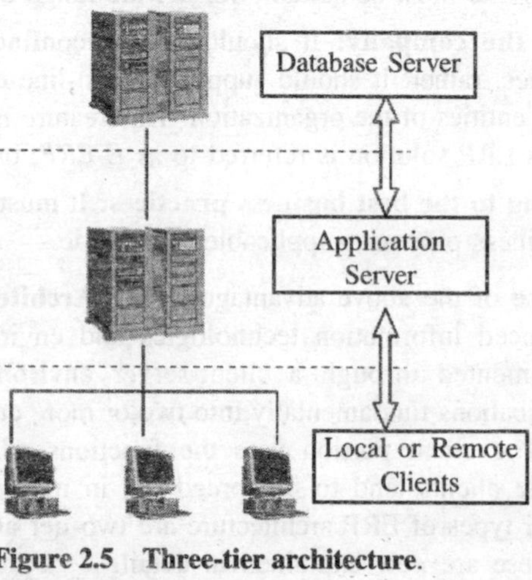

Figure 2.5 Three-tier architecture.

As we have seen from the above discussions, any ERP Architecture has to be designed for three basic functional areas:

(i) **Database.** The central repository for all the data transferred to and from the client.

(ii) **Clients.** Here raw data gets inputted, request for information is submitted, and data satisfying this request are presented.

(iii) **Application component.** Acts as an intermediary between the client and the database.

The next level elements of ERP Architecture are:

- Repository
- GUI driver
- Logic server
- DB driver
- Database administration
- Operating system

Figure 2.6 provides pictorial view of these elements.

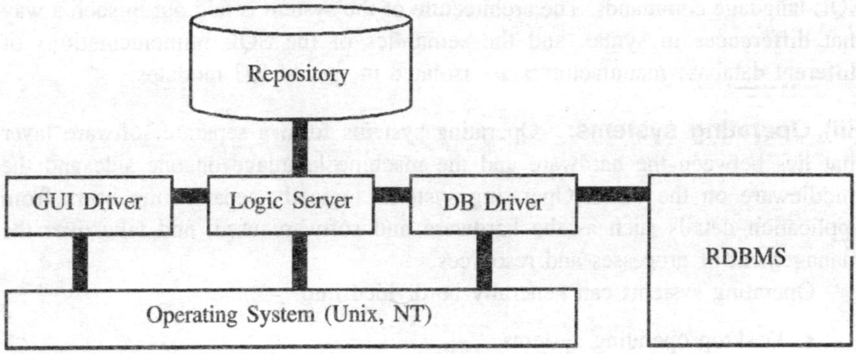

Figure 2.6 Elements in ERP architecture.

We will discuss a few of these elements in detail.

(i) Graphical user interfaces: Manufacturers design Graphical User Interfaces (GUI) according to certain style guides, in which the interface model and the design of windows, menus, operating elements, and system messages are determined.

The familiar style guides are:

- CUA—Common User Access (IBM)
- Human Interface Guidelines (Apple)
- OSF/Motif Style Guide (OSF)
- Windows Interface (Microsoft)

All the style guides listed are first and foremost technical manuals and do not focus sufficiently enough on ergonomic design of graphical user interfaces. This aspect must therefore be addressed in supplement documents. For example, SAP has developed the SAP style guide on the basis of the style guides listed. The uniformity achieved with the help of the SAP style guide affects all parts of the interface design, i.e. online help, control elements, menus, toolbars and pushbutton bar, etc.

(ii) RDBMS: As a rule, business applications work with large amounts of data. Master data and transaction data often take up many gigabytes of disk storage. To be able to handle such data volumes comfortably, powerful storage and access methods are required. *Relational Database Management Systems (RDBMS)* are characterized by their logical simplicity because they stores data as well as show the relations between the data in two-dimensional tables. Every table has a primary key by which table entries can be uniquely identified.

Access to the data stored in a relational database takes place with simple, largely self-explanatory expressions that follow the SQL standard. Further, end users and application programmers have the ability to access the subset of stored data relevant to them, using predefined, external views, independent of predefined access paths and the internal table organization.

For the definition and manipulation of data, the R/3 system exclusively uses SQL language commands. The architecture of the system is laid out in such a way that differences in syntax and the semantics of the SQL implementations of different database manufacturers are isolated in special R/3 modules.

(iii) Operating systems: Operating systems form a separate software layer that lies between the hardware and the machine language on one side and the middleware on the other. Operating systems logically separate the users from application details such as the hardware and software used, and take over the management of processes and resources.

Operating systems can generally be divided into:

- Desktop operating systems
- Server operating systems

(a) Desktop operating systems. These are single user operating systems that run on user's personal computers and are optimized for supporting individual applications such as word processors and spreadsheet programs. Typical examples are MS-DOS with Windows 95 and Macintosh Operating System.

(b) Server operating systems. These are installed on powerful, centralized computers that give access to the resources of these computers to many users and applications.

Repository: The repository environment contains the complete set of the metadata of a business. It is globally accessible. As compared to a data dictionary, the repository environment not only contains an expanded set of metadata, but it can also be implemented across multiple hardware platforms and database management systems.

We will now discuss the actual design and architecture of popular ERP brands.

Architecture Overview of SAP R/3 ERP

The R/3 System is based on software-oriented, multiplayer client/server architecture. For this reason, the R/3 system has a modular structure with methods for controlling relationship between individual software components.

The structure of the R/3 system follows a layer model with largely independent function layers connected by interfaces. The main layers are:

- Basis layer
- Application layer

The basis layer contains the middleware of the R/3 system. This middleware makes the applications independent of the system interfaces and the operating system, database system, and communication system used, and ensures optimal handling of the business transactions.

On the basis layer sits the application layer, which implements the business functions and processes of the R/3 system.

Architecture Overview of Baan's ERP

The architecture and technology of Baan's ERP solution offers the benefits of open architecture and independence from related technologies (database, operating system, user interface, network, middleware, and application management systems). It offers broad-based compliance with industry standards in a scalable solution. Baan has been a pioneer in creating components that are independent of middleware layers, operating systems and hardware platforms, proprietary information APIs, and even application management systems. It basically consists of three layers:

- Presentation layer
- Application layer
- Database layer.

Baan has developed an open implementation of Simplified OSI model in which the application layer consists of a hardware/UI/database dependent part (called the porting set) and a hardware/UI/database independent part (the BAAN 4GL code).

The logic server (bshell) controls the application process. The application is written in 4GL and compiled to objects. This object, together with the data dictionary, which defines the data models in the applications, is called the *BAAN application*. Each user has his own display driver, logic server, and database server processes.

With this architecture, Baan is very flexible in supporting different hardware platforms, user interfaces and databases by writing a specific driver for the user interfaces and/or databases. In BAAN ERP, there are two supported user interfaces:

- Microsoft display driver
- Windows 95/NT

The following databases are supported in Baan ERP:

- DB2/6000
- DB2/390
- Informix 7
- Oracle 7/8
- Sybase
- Microsoft SQL Server

Cost of ERP

The cost of ERP typically includes costs of hardware, software, training, data conversion and reengineering.

Hardware, though costly, is a one-time cost. Hardware typically includes computers, servers, peripherals, network cables, hubs, etc. The decision makers have to decide on implementing the best and the most sophisticated hardware possible, at the same time keeping a balance with the costs so that the investment certainly results in benefits in the long run.

Software includes the range of different ERP packages available in the market. The cost of software would vary greatly on the ERP brand or vendor, the functionalities it covers, special options available, competitors markets, and so on. Some of the common packages available are Oracle, SAP, Baan, etc. We will be discussing the individual packages in detail in Chapter 4.

Training cost is not only the cost of training the people to operate the software but also the cost of correcting the mistakes while performing the job in ERP. Secondly, the person using ERP has to adapt a whole new process to get used to ERP. Quite often, it takes a year for people to learn this, which may have considerable impact on bottom line of the organization.

Data conversion includes costs in moving corporate information such as customer and supplier records, product design data, etc. from the old system to the new ERP system. These costs will generally be higher for enterprises that haven't managed their data efficiently and concisely. Most of the time, companies prefer to use some middle-level software to append the data into the ERP system. Those costs have to be considered as migration costs.

Reengineering, as the name suggests, is a process of engineering everything again. As a result, it comprises a majority of the total cost of implementing ERP. It typically includes consultancy charges, process change costs, costs of removal of old policies and practices. Cost of ERP should not be viewed as an expense but an investment towards an ability that provides better profitability, market share or customer service through integration and automation.

EXERCISES

1. Explain with examples the conceptual model of ERP and its evolution.
2. What is the difference between MRP software and MRP module of ERP?
3. Discuss various elements of ERP architecture.
4. Search for basic architecture of J.D. Edwards and Mfg/Pro.
5. How is the cost of ERP implementation is built up?

CHAPTER 3

The Best Practices in ERP

One of the definitions of ERP is "the amalgamation of world-class (best) practices together".

It is said that, if ERP is implemented successfully, the company *automatically* becomes world class in terms of its practices. This statement is true for most of the ERP products. In fact, it is observed that *lesser the flexibility* in the ERP product, more the chances of becoming world class (but unfortunately lesser the chances of success).

We will discuss this in detail in Chapter 6. Here we will analyze the recommended best practices in ERP.

THE CONCEPT OF BEST PRACTICE

Right from the industrial revolution and even further, we can see the efforts put in to improve existing practices. Typically, the classical industrial engineering principle says: *there is always a better method available than the existing*. Here the 'better' ultimately means improved *efficiency, effectiveness* and *economics.* If we understand the motto of this principle deeply, we may find the basic motivation of the *kaizen* in it. In fact, this principle clearly supports the view that nothing is the best forever.

In this context, let us see what is the best practice in ERP environment. ERP assumes the fundamental set-ups as explained in Chapter 2 as "Pillars of ERP". The best practice in ERP then can be defined as the utilization of these set-ups to the maximum possible to produce the desired performance in terms of *customer focus, zero waste of all the resources, and value creation.* Tangibly, it leads to increase in quality and service, and reduction of cost and response time.

ERP enjoys having a strong skeleton based on these best practices. All the workflows in ERP are so thoughtfully maintained that it ensures that the user automatically follows the best practice. It won't allow the user to bypass or modify the predetermined course of actions that may create *non-value added activity*.

We will now discuss these best practices in logical sequence.

STYLE OF MANUFACTURING

We can classify various industries as shown in the Figure 3.1 into different sectors. This analysis of industrial typology brings into focus the critical parameters of each type by comparing their different requirements, and thus helps understand the overall fitness of the organization in the category of world-class practices.

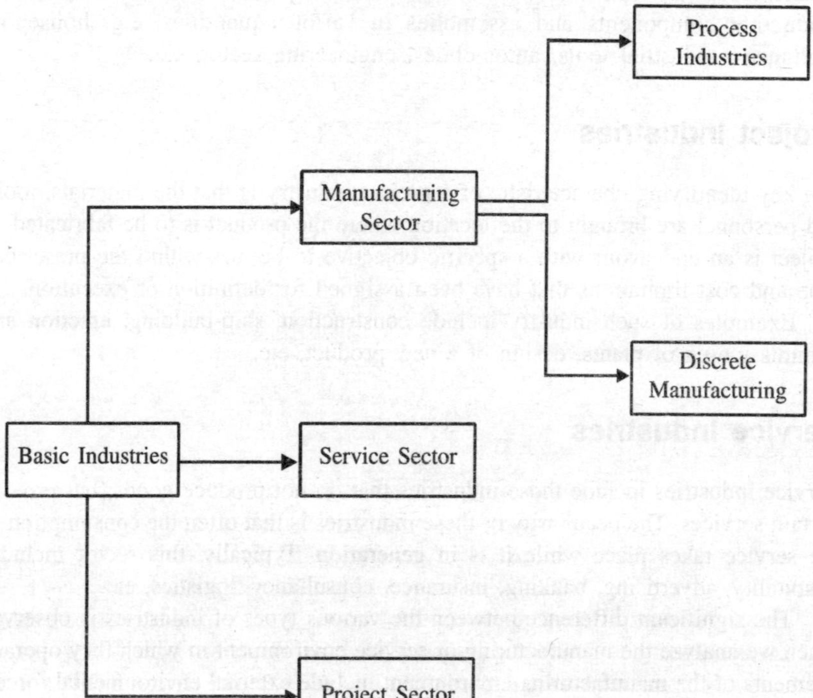

Figure 3.1 Different industrial sectors.

Manufacturing Industries

These are the industries engaged in the production of goods (finished products) that have value in the marketplace. These industries are further classified into the following two categories.

(i) Process industries (Flow production or continuous process production industries): Process manufacturing is defined as the production that adds value by mixing, separating, forming and/or performing chemical reactions. It may be either batch or continuous node. These industries manufacture highly standardized non-discrete products in extremely large volumes using a continuous process. Process manufacturing is characterized by wet or dry product flow measurable by weight or volume, small WIP and short lead times. Examples of such industries could be beverage, cement, chemicals, etc.

(ii) Discrete manufacturing industries: Discrete, countable products and component parts characterize discrete manufacturing. A feature of this type of production process is that it produces a single component or unit of product each time an operation is performed. Discrete part products can be disassembled and reassembled. This type of manufacturing entails the production of discrete units of production components and assemblies in various quantities, e.g. household appliances, industrial tools, automobiles, engineering sector, etc.

Project Industries

The key identifying characteristic of a project industry is that the materials, tools, and personnel are brought to the location where the product is to be fabricated. A project is an endeavour with a specific objective to be met within the prescribed time and cost limitations that have been assigned for definition or execution.

Examples of such industry include construction, ship-building, erection and commissioning of plants, design of a new product, etc.

Service Industries

Service industries include those industries that do not produce goods, but provide certain services. The peculiarity of these industries is that often the consumption of the service takes place while it is in generation. Typically, this sector includes hospitality, advertising, banking, insurance, consultancy, logistics, etc.

The significant difference between the various types of industries is observed when we analyze the manufacturing or service environment in which they operate. Elements of the manufacturing environment include external environmental forces, corporate strategy, business unit strategy, other functional strategies (marketing, engineering, finance, etc.), product selection, product/process design, product/process technology, and management of competencies. Ultimately, what matters is the framework in which the overall manufacturing or service strategy is developed and implemented. To understand the basic theme behind this framework, we will discuss the concept of customer order Decoupling Point.

Concept of Customer Order Decoupling Point (CODP): The CODP is the point that indicates how deeply the customer order penetrates into the supply chain. It is the distinction between the order-driven and forecast-driven parts of the supply chain for a particular product market combination. Items that are kept in stock at the CODP are those items for which demand must be forecast due to the fact that future demand between the moment of release of items and the moment those items are received is (partially) unknown; the lead time of supplying the item is longer than the lead time requested by the customer. Downstream of the CODP, items are not kept in stock since future demand for these items between release moments and receipt moments is known; the lead time of supplying the item from the CODP to the customer is shorter than the lead time requested by the customer. Demand at the CODP is independent demand, either originating directly from the demand forecast of end products (Make-to-Stock), demand forecasts of modules (Assemble-to-Order), or of components (Make-to-Order). All releases downstream of the CODP are based on actual customer orders and hence are not planned under uncertainty of demand. All releases upstream of the CODP are planned based on dependent demand. In production logistics, it is common to introduce decoupling points if production lead times are much longer than the acceptable order lead times in the market and/or where there is significant change in market risk. This is the point where upstream activities are no longer driven by a customer order, but they are driven by customer order prognosis.

Based on the CODP concept the different types of environments are often referred to whether these relate to a company, plant, product, or service for make-to-stock, assemble-to-order, make-to-order, or engineer-to-order. These are discussed now.

Make-to-stock. Refers to a production environment where products can be and usually are finished before receipt of a customer order. Customer orders are typically filled from existing stock, and production orders are used to replenish those stocks. This is typically mass manufacturing with pushing the sales philosophy. Figure 3.2 illustrates this concept.

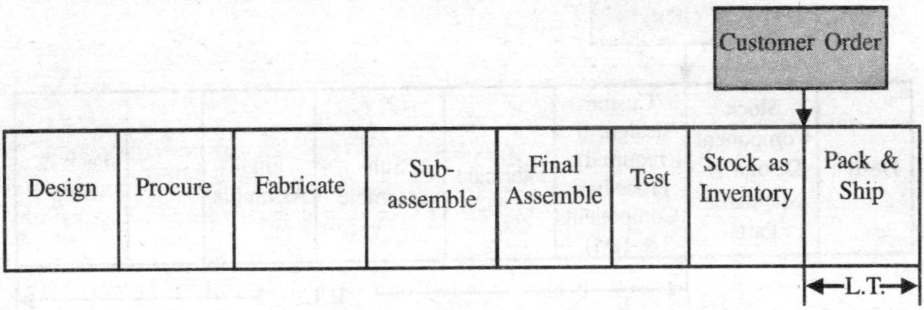

Figure 3.2 Make-to-stock.

Assemble-to-order (Configure/Finish-to-order). Denotes a production environment where goods or service can be assembled after receipt of a customer's order. The key components (bulk, semi-finished, intermediate, subassembly, fabricated, purchased, packaging, etc.) used in the assembly or finishing process are planned and possibly stocked in anticipation of a customer order. Receipt of an order initiates assembly of the customized product. This strategy is useful where a large number of end products (based on the selection of options and accessories) can be assembled from common components. Figure 3.3 illustrates this concept.

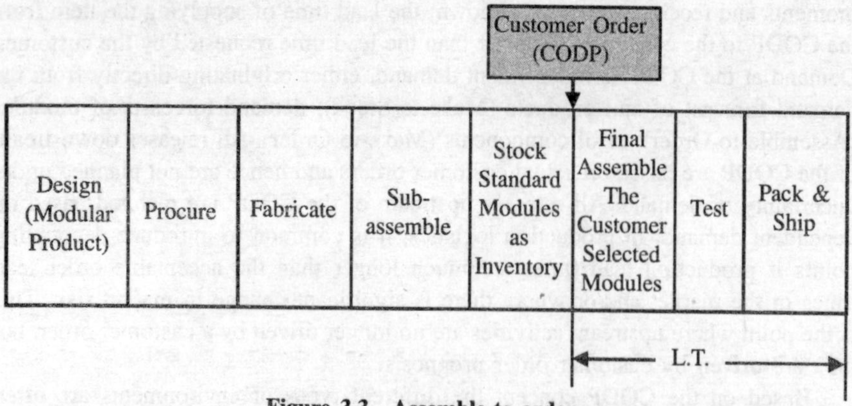

Figure 3.3 Assemble-to-order.

Make-to-order. In this environment, goods or service can be manufactured/offered after receipt of a customer's order. The final product is usually a combination of standard items and items custom-designed to meet the special needs of the customer. This gives more options (as compared to assemble-to-order) to the customers in design, aesthetics, utility, accessories, etc. Figure 3.4 illustrates this concept.

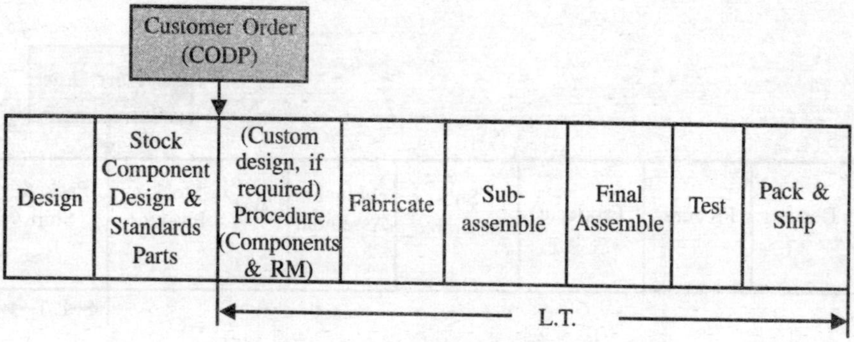

Figure 3.4 Make-to-order.

Design-to-order (Engineer-to-order). This is a highly customer focus environment where the individual customer gives product specifications that require unique engineering design, significant customization in manufacturing, or even new purchased materials. Each customer order results in a unique set of part numbers, bills of material, and routings. Figure 3.5 illustrates this concept.

The recommended practice of manufacturing by ERP is the Assemble-to-order or Make-to-order. In fact, the ERP concept is the best fit for these environments. It is irrelevant for Make-to-stock environment and does not support the complete requirements of Engineer-to-order scenario. We will see in detail the reasoning of these views in Chapter 7.

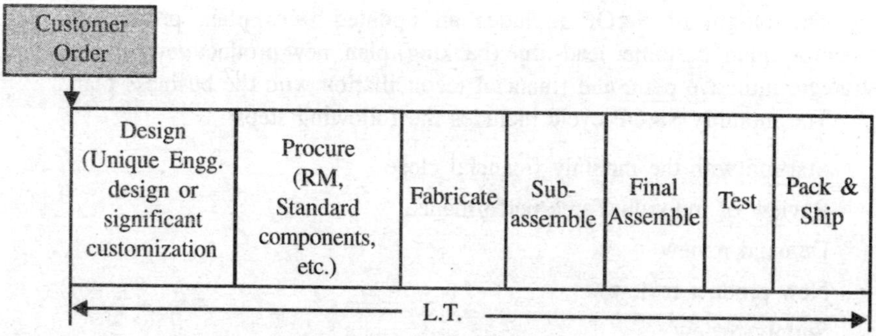

Figure 3.5 Engineer-to-order.

DEMAND MANAGEMENT

The recommended best practice of demand estimation in ERP is the Sales and Operations Planning (S&OP). As we have seen, ERP assumes integrated views of all the concerned process owners, and S&OP is the suggested methodology for achieving these demand plans for the integrated organizational requirements. S&OP ultimately results in Master Production Schedule (MPS), which will further trigger the lower level materials demand through Materials Requirement Planning (MRP).

We will now discuss S&OP in detail with industrial applications.

Sales and Operations Planning

To state most generally, S&OP is a business process responsible for bringing all information sources to the attentions of those at the helm of business affairs. The crux of the process is to have all the data in its latest form available to the decision maker.

The definition of S&OP given by *APICS* is:

> Sales and Operations is the process of establishing production rates which will achieve management objective in terms of raising or lowering inventories or backlogs, while usually attempting to keep the production force relatively stable.

Sales and operations planning facilitates cooperation between manufacturing, quality control, engineering and/or development, finance, sales and marketing by coordinating their respective plans. S&OP is an integrated management planning and control process. And it is because of this that it is continually used to achieve the *synchronization and alignment* of all the functional plans of the organization. It regularly and routinely reviews customer demand and supply resources and "re-plans" across a rolling planning horizon (typically 12–18 months). The replanning process occurs at least monthly. The plan helps the management understand the performance level and thus they can evaluate themselves.

The output of S&OP includes an updated sales plan, production plan, inventory plan, customer lead-time (backlog) plan, new product development plan, strategic initiative plan, and financial reconciliation with the business plan.

The monthly S&OP cycle includes the following steps:

Starting with the monthly financial close
Review of individual area performance
Demand review
New product review
Supply review
Resource validation
Finance review
Strategic review
Final executive review and approval.

A key to a "best practice" S&OP process is that the process is demand driven. The questions posed for the sales and operations are mainly driven by the market, which include questions like what are we committed to sell, how much selling is there, what are the repercussions of change in plan this time, etc. From this anticipated demand forecast, supply resource priorities and plans are developed. There could be variations or changes in the plans or forecasts of the months, which are solved by incorporating changes in the next month plans. Demand, supply, and inventory are balanced and synchronized during each planning cycle.

S&OP starts with a series of monthly meetings with middle management performing what is called pre-SOP during which the current plans are compared against the previous plans and all the differences are accounted for future course of action. Thus, while looking at the overall strategic plan of the organization, S&OP coordinates the plans of the various departments.

As mentioned earlier, S&OP is usually a monthly plan, as compared to MPS which is a weekly/daily, or strategic business plan which is annual. It can thus be said that S&OP is a medium range planning. The initiation of S&OP is through the Sales and Marketing department, which compares the actual demand with the sales plan and reaches a specific future demand. This information is then percolated to the manufacturing, engineering and finance departments. If the other departments cannot accept the marketing plan, then the marketing plan itself has to be adjusted. As such, S&OP is called *Game Planning* with respect to the overall context in which trade offs are made. Also, SOP can be stated both in the rupee terms or aggregate units of output per month. Figure 3.6 shows the overall planning flow in S&OP framework as discussed above.

The company's senior management creates this plan and the main inputs are the forecast or marketing plan, the long-term or strategic plan, and the budget or financial plan. The production plan is defined in time periods (months and quarters). It is the monthly portion of this plan that the senior management hands over to the master scheduler to turn into the master production schedule. The national marketing forecast when balanced against the regional sales forecast is

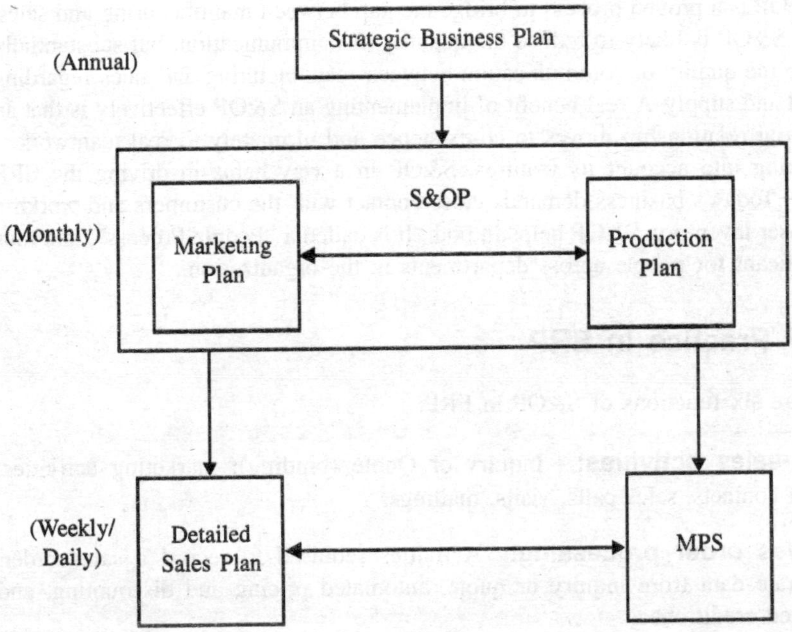

Figure 3.6 S&OP framework.

one of the key inputs. This, together with the long-term business plan, establishes the numbers required by family group for the plan. The financial plan is then a schedule of the cash flow and profit by period based on the planned activity derived from the other two plans. The result of the management sorting out and testing these numbers against the resources available is the sales and operations plan.

Significance and Advantages of S&OP

The S&OP is management's statement of intention and is the master scheduler's authority to organize the use of the capacity and the supply of material to meet the plan. It also provides the means of comparing resources available against those required, and this check is carried out by using resource requirements planning—an interactive what-if module. The plan takes into account the fact that forecasts and plans can vary and, therefore, a provision is made for adjustments. This, difference is taken into account by storing the well-determined level of extra finished goods.

The significant benefits achieved through effective S&OP are:

- Increased forecast accuracy
- Reduced inventories
- Improved lead times
- Increased constraint visibility

S&OP is a proven process to bridge the gap between manufacturing and sales. In fact, S&OP is likely to reduce the quantity of communication, but substantially increase the quality of communication between manufacturing and sales regarding demand and supply. A real benefit of implementing an S&OP effectively is that an adversarial relationship moves to co-existence and ultimately to real teamwork.

Taking into account its features, S&OP in a way helps in driving the ERP strategy. Today's business demands close contact with the customers and working with lesser inventory, S&OP helps in both. It is called a "People Process", and thus is significant for people across departments in the organization.

S&OP Practice in ERP

There are six functions of S&OP in ERP:

(i) Pre-sales activities: Inquiry or Quote (binding), marketing activities, tracking contacts, sales calls, visits, mailings.

(ii) Sales order processing: Activities required to record a sales order, incorporate data from inquiry or quote, automated pricing and discounting, and automated credit check.

(iii) Inventory sourcing: Check of inventory, orders and production to see if order can be delivered when the customer desires, includes shipping and considers weekends/holidays.

(iv) Delivery: Releasing documents to warehouse to initiate pick, pack and ship; sequenced and grouped for warehouse operation efficiency; the materials management module carries out picking, packing and shipping.

(v) Billing: Sales order data copied to invoice; can be printed and mailed, faxed or transmitted electronically; accounting records updated.

(vi) Payment: Payment may be physical check or electronic; cash debited and customer account credited; quick processing avoids credit check problems.

In terms of breakdown of the functions, the S&OP process includes:

- Complete initial forecast
- Complete forecast review
- Load to ERP
- Capacity review
- Sales and operations planning meeting
- Adjust and reload to ERP.

We will now discuss the case studies on S&OP modules in ERP brands and S&OP practices of a few leading companies in the world.

ADEXA SOLUTIONS

Adexa is a leading brand which provides sales and operations planning solutions. It integrates forecasting, demand-planning, inventory optimization, material and capacity planning, and supply planning into a unified environment.

The following are the features of the solution provided by Adexa:

- Reduced lead times
- Profitable deployment of inventory across the enterprise
- Synchronization of material planning, capacity planning and allocation planning
- Improvement of service levels
- Less expediting costs
- Optimization of safety stock and raw material levels.

SAP R/3

Figures 3.7(a) and 3.7(b) show the S&OP module in the SAP R/3 solution.

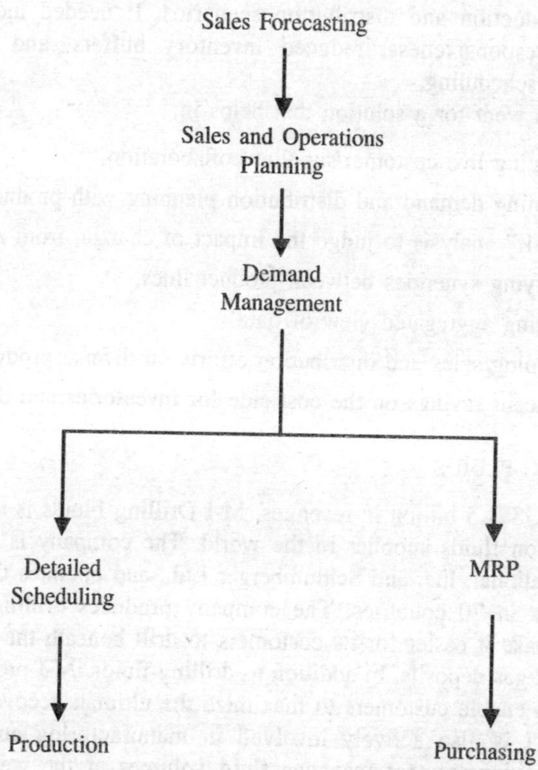

Figure 3.7(a) Sales and operations planning approach in SAP R/3.

Sales and Operations Planning	Jan.	Feb.	March	April	May	June
1. Sales Forecast						
2. Production Plan						
3. Stock Level						
4. Working Days						
5. Capacity (Shipping Cases)						
6. Utilization						
7. NRG-A (cases)						
8. NRG-B (cases)						

Figure 3.7(b) Sales and operations planning screen in SAP R/3.

HINDUSTAN LEVER LIMITED

The number of markets served by HLL required the development of flexible planning, production and distribution scenarios. It needed increased supplier/distribution responsiveness, reduced inventory buffers, and optimization of planning and scheduling.

HLL thus went for a solution that helps in:

- facilitating live customer/supplier collaboration,
- integrating demand and distribution planning with production schedule,
- "what-If" analysis to judge the impact of change, from any source,
- identifying synergies between product lines,
- providing aggregated view of data,
- combining sales and distribution efforts on diverse product lines, and
- significant savings on the cost side for inventories and distribution.

M-I DRILLING FLUIDS

With nearly US$1.5 billion in revenues, M-I Drilling Fluids is the largest drilling and completion fluids supplier in the world. The company is owned jointly by Smith International, Inc. and Schlumberger Ltd., and operates through more than 300 locations in 70 countries. The company produces drilling and completion fluids that make it easier for its customers to drill beneath the earth's surface to reach oil and gas deposits. In addition to drilling fluids, M-I produces completion fluids, which enable customers to maximize the ultimate recovery of oil and gas reserves. M-I is also actively involved in manufacturing and servicing fluid processing equipment that manages fluid volumes at the well site as well as managing the fluid wastes after drilling operations have ceased.

In this highly dynamic and competitive industry, the key to M-I's success has been its ability to understand customers' changing needs, and to measure its ability to deliver value. More than 10 years back, the group developed a model to forecast its customers' expenditures in drilling and completion operations. This solution models the cyclical nature of the oil and gas business. For example, as oil and gas prices drive M-I's customers to increase their spending and activity, their growing demands on the supply sector can sow the seeds of decline in the industry.

The output of this model drives our annual business planning process — setting common expectations about the industry environment we will encounter in the coming year. In addition to this model, M-I recently completed work on a monthly regional model of drilling activity that is used in its Sales and Operations Planning (SOP) to forecast product demand where that demand is statistically related to the level of drilling.

This econometric approach was used to provide 'out-months' forecasting with a shorter, more detailed forecasting approach for the first two months of the forecast period. One of the main reasons to build this application was to reconcile the industry view, with our operational planning. The SOP did a short- to intermediate-term forecast, and allowed optimization of purchasing and logistics functions, and provided 100 per cent customer service level at lower cost.

From the above discussion, it is very clear that S&OP results in feasible, workable and naturally optimistic plans that ensure the perfect allocations of all the organization resources, thus achieving maximum possible returns.

It is expected in the ERP environment that the organization sincerely follow the S&OP process to estimate the demands of finished goods or any other sellable goods. Then ERP will generate MPS which gives the detailed plan for the manufacturing. The organization ideally has to respect the MPS recommendations and should not deviate from it. It provides enough flexibility to change or replan the MPS recommendations. Hence, ideally the user should operate through the system than outside the system. This will ensure that all the benefits of S&OP process are passed through without any losses in terms of inventory, service level, expenses, time, and so on.

MRP is the next demand estimation engine, which provides the detailed procurement and production requirements in quantities and time. All the *lower level items* must be managed through MRP module of ERP.

The best practice of demand management, which is incorporated in ERP, is visible through MPS and MRP modules. To receive its full benefits, one must respect the MPS and MRP recommendations for all the materials requirements of the organization. It clearly assumes that the organization *must* include all the items in these modules, including spare parts (both sellable and internally required), consumables, utility materials, stationary items, tooling, etc., besides the finished goods, work in progress, packing materials, and raw materials. It in turn assumes the best practices already in place in the organization, namely, customer-supplier integration, zero defects, Total Quality Management (TQM), Total Productive Maintenance (TPM), accurate budgeting, etc.

In fact, the best practice ERP assumes regarding the inventory management is "Inventory can be controlled only at the materials requisition level, i.e. before its birth, than its physical arrival when it just can't be controlled but becomes *post-mortem.*" Hence the ERP concept does not recommend a menu where the user can manually create indents or material requisition, but the same must come as system recommendations.

Regarding the project items where normally the requirements are not known in their fullest specifications before their need, one should control the inventory by carefully studying such items in terms of their demand and supply patterns, and establish a statistical inventory model, which can be further incorporated into ERP, thus making the whole planning process feasible and integrated.

ORGANIZATION STRUCTURE AND ELEMENTS

ERP believes that the organization is a **lean enterprise** where friction between the various departments is absent. In fact, it assumes that the whole organization has the primary objective of specifying exactly the value for its customer and then organizing the same. This definition of value is the same for all the employees in the organization, thus avoiding the normal tendency to define value differently to favour its own role in providing it. For example, typically in non-lean organization, the manufacturer may think the physical product itself is the customer's primary interest, whereas the sales and service department thinks that the responsive customer relations account for most of the value perceived by the customer. This lack of understanding the value definition ultimately leads to divergence in the performance of the individuals that causes overall chaos and unhealthy atmosphere in the organization. Hence world-class practice believes in the **common language** within the organization. This culture is predominantly observed in lean enterprises, thus resulting in the best fit for the ERP environment.

Moreover, a lean organization has detailed specifications of all the actions (for resource requirements) required to bring a product from concept to launch, from order to delivery, and from raw materials to finished product that goes into the hands of the customer and throughout its useful life. This takes care of perfect and complete data sets availability to load into ERP for accurate estimations and recommendations.

The lean organization believes in absolutely flat organization structure with empowered employees. The structure is purely based on **process**, and not at all on functions. Every business process or subprocess exists to provide a needed product or service for a defined customer. These products and services are produced within the process according to the defined requirements, rules, or constraints. The process requires materials and information, which are provided by suppliers, and consumes the resources allocated to the process. Since ERP conceptually integrates the processes and not the functions, this process-based culture is the primary criteria for ERP fitness. The main job of ERP in such environment is to **replace** all these processes into a seamless flow of information.

ERP thus provides authority of getting all the information about the organization to all the users (ideally all the employees). No constraint like confidentiality, hierarchy, or authority exists. Hence the right of information seeking is never questioned. Every employee is motivated to browse, analyze and comment on the performance of the organization through the ERP system. Thus ERP expects an employee to be much more matured and accountable resource of the organization. For example, ERP calls traditional purchase person as *Buyer*. A buyer is expected to be having four types of skills:

1. Technical skills: He should understand what he is buying, what is the alternative to that, what are its end applications, etc.

2. Commercial skills: He should know what are the legal implications in terms of costs, licenses, and procedures, etc. attached to the item he buys.

3. Negotiation skills: This does not mean only to reduce purchase prices but goes beyond to improve supplier relationships, long-term contracts, determining variations in costs, transactional process integrations, etc.

4. Integrated planning skills: The buyer is expected to know the overall impact of his daily decisions on working capital, inventory, customer service level, production efficiency, maintenance, etc.

ERP assumes this type of empowered people as users and then further helps them take accurate and cost effective decisions in their daily transactions and planning. The best practice of ERP here could be to share all the information of the organization to the entire set of users without any obstacles to facilitate both productive and best mixes of planning decisions.

ACTIVITY BASED COSTING (ABC)

Activity based costing can be considered as the backbone of the ERP concept. The whole idea of ERP is to estimate the **total activity costs** for a particular customer order. In fact, the best practice in ERP is to estimate the revenues and allocate the expenses for a particular order. Thus, ERP will help in planning accurately the margin per customer order. The main principle behind this is the **target costing.** We can also say in industrial engineering language that *ABC is a method that provides Therbligs for costing.*

Let us discuss this technique in detail to understand the concept of ERP. Activity based costing can be defined as a methodology that measures the cost and performance of the activities. Proper resources are assigned to activities. The activities are then assigned to cost objects based on their use. In the process, the system recognizes the casual relationship of cost drivers to activities, thus showing the real performance picture.

Activity based cost analysis is different from traditional concepts in a number of ways. The concept of Activity based costing lies in the fact that costs should be planned for and managed *before* they are incurred, rather than simply monitored and controlled *after* the event.

The initial objective is to understand the activities that are performed throughout the organization and to estimate the costs associated with delivering those activities. Then the causes of these costs, called *cost drivers*, can be identified to provide information, which is very useful in decision-making. Activity based costing attempts to address the real issues of how and why costs are incurred and does not, therefore, simply record the expenditure and then allocate it arbitrarily to cost centres or products. Traditionally, financial accounting provided external information to shareholders, authorities, creditors and other stakeholders, and is unsuitable for internal decision-making. Hence the limitations of financial accounting are that it analyzes profitability by department or cost centre and costs by category or type of expense. A large proportion of costs are allocated to overheads and, therefore, complete control over costs is lost.

Activity based costing enables the management to utilize cost information for the purpose of decision making at all levels and focus on how the decisions will affect the overall profitability of the company. To summarize, Activity based costing includes:

- Providing a way of assessing why costs are incurred, rather than how much is incurred.
- Forming a basis of controlling costs by monitoring the underlying causes.
- Providing a basis for aligning costs with activities as a means of focusing attention on cost management.

Basic ABC Principles

Though ABC is thought of as a complex procedure, the following basic principles allow us to understand it in much simpler terms.

PRINCIPLE 1: ***Activities consume resources.*** The more an activity is performed, the more resources will be consumed by it.

PRINCIPLE 2: ***Activities have a cause.*** All activity is performed for a reason or cause.

PRINCIPLE 3: ***Customers, products, or channels cause different levels of activity.*** Traditional costing methods, such as standard or absorption costing, allocate base costs directly to products, customers or distribution channels. These methods ignore the principle that resources are actually consumed by activities, and not by the products, customers and channels. Activity based costing allocates costs to customers, products and channels in line with the proportion of activity they actually consume.

Table 3.1 shows how ABC can be used to view the correct allocations of costs in warehouse operation management. The left table shows the traditional costing approach where all the costs are divided into various accounting heads, whereas the right table shows various activities that are required for warehouse operations. This will help the organization in determining the non-value added activities and to plan its resources better.

Thus the goal of ABC is to increase value-added activities while minimizing the time and money spent on non-value added activities. It changes the focus of costing to manage activities, as opposed to managing rupees. ABC identifies the key activities performed in all stages of delivering the product or service to the customer. These are the activities that consume the resource and these are the same activities that create product. Recognizing this relationship is the cornerstone of ABC. It allocates cost (or resources) to activities based on consumption of resources (i.e., resource cost assignment).

Table 3.1 Example of ABC Application

Warehouse Budget (Rs)	
Labour	2,50,000
Fringes	70,000
Supplies	50,000
Depreciation	60,000
Other	32,000
Total	**Rs. 4,62,000**

Warehouse Activities	
Receive Material	Rs. 92,000
Pick Material	50,000
Store Material	46,000
Deliver Parts	46,000
Housekeeping	41,000
Inspect Material	42,000
Expedite Material	25,000
Search for Lost Parts	70,000
Supervision	50,000
Total	**Rs. 4,62,000**

Elements of ABC

The following are key definitions used in ABC:

Activity: *Work performed within an organization.* The aggregations of actions performed within organizations that are useful for purposes of activity-based costing. *Example:* activity of processing an order over the telephone: the actual process of taking the order.

Activity driver: *Associates activities with their respective cost object.* Activity drivers measure the frequency and intensity of the demand placed on activities by cost objects. They are typically a one-to-one relationship with the activity. *Example:* activity driver in processing an order over the telephone: number of minutes per telephone call.

Activity measure: *A measure of the workload involved in the activity.* Can be similar to the activity driver. *Example:* activity measure in processing an order over the telephone: number of orders taken.

Bill of activities: *A listing of the activities required* (and, optionally, the associated cost of the resources consumed) *by a product or other cost object.* It should list each activity, activity drivers, number of units, unit cost per driver and extended cost that, taken together, compose the total for any particular cost object.

Cost drivers: *Any element that would cause a change in the cost of an activity. Example:* cost driver in processing an order over the telephone: frequency.

Cost element: *An amount paid for a resource consumed by an activity and included in an activity cost pool.*
Example: cost element in processing an order over the telephone: general ledger account containing wages of the telephone order clerk.

Cost object: Any customer, product, service, contract, project, or other work unit for which a separate cost measurement is desired. *Example:* cost object in processing an order over the telephone—the customer.

Performance measures: Indicators of the work performed and the results achieved in an activity, process, or organizational unit. Performance measures may be financial or operational. *Examples* performance measure in processing an order over the telephone—sales revenue volume per unit of time.

Process: A series of activities that are linked to perform a specific objective. *Example:* processing an order over the telephone—entering an order into the system and passing it onto production planning.

Resource: An economic element applied or used in the performance of activities. Salaries and materials are resources used in the performance of activities. They can also include any non-monetary assets which are essential for the completion of the item. *Example:* resources in processing an order over the telephone—wages of the telephone order clerk, maintenance on telephones used, office supplies needed to complete the order.

Resource driver: A measurement tool to associate costs with their respective activities or cost objects. Resource drivers measure the quantity of resources consumed by an activity, typically a one-to-one relationship with the resource. *Example:* resource driver in processing an order over the telephone—amount of office supplies used per call or number of items sold per call.

As discussed above, the ERP concept is developed on the ABC concept combined with standard approach to cost estimation.

COSTING METHODS

ERP strongly recommends ABC based costing methods, preferably standard costing or landed cost approach. It never recommends the traditional methods of LIFO, FIFO, and Weighted Average, etc., which existed mainly because powerful systems like ERP were not in the picture. In fact, ERP looks at LIFO and FIFO more as material issue policy than the costing method. Even ideally, FIFO is the only method to be followed for the material issue policy in ERP environment because of the in-built world class manufacturing philosophy where inventory is seen more as a liability and never as an asset.

George Plossl, in his theory of manufacturing, has analyzed the basic mindset behind best practices discussed above. According to him, it can be viewed as a functional summary of all the best practices capsuled in a world-class ERP product. Thus:

- Production problems must and can be eliminated. They cannot be covered up successfully with cushions of inventory and time.
- Inventory is more of a liability than an asset, having real value only when it is flowing through operations or used to support them.

- Tolerating some downtime while striving to eliminate their causes is better than preventing idle time by manufacturing items not required immediately.
- More frequent and precise replanning, such as computing daily, rather than weekly, does not make it more accurate.
- Replanning is admitting failure; it is not a substitute for sound execution.
- Plans impossible to execute are absolutely worthless.
- Lead times can not only be monitored and adjusted but can also be controlled.
- Reducing set-up time is worth the effort.
- Planning defines resources needed to make what is planned; execution applies available resources to make what customers want now.
- Only resources requiring long periods for actions should be planned ahead; detailed plans should cover only very short horizons.
- There is one manufacturing planning and control system framework common to all types of manufacturing.
- All employees need continuous education.

Even though the above guidelines apparently look applicable to operations management, the themes are applicable to all the functionalities of the organization. The basic functional architectural design and the coding framework of ERP *should* respect the above guidelines to build world-class product.

EXERCISES

1. Define the term 'Best Practice' in ERP context.
2. Why S&OP is regarded as the key functionality of ERP culture?
3. What are the major differences between service and manufacturing organization?
4. What are the practical difficulties faced in generating all the material requisitions through ERP? How should one overcome these problems?
5. Why is ERP concept more suitable to Lean organizations?
6. 'ABC is the backbone of ERP'. Comment.

CHAPTER 4 ERP Vendor Analysis

INTRODUCTION

In Chapter 3 we have seen a few basic principles (best practices) of the ERP concept. Now let us analyze the *tools for ERP* which are nothing but the ERP products available in the market. We find today a number of players offering ERP suite of products. Popular examples of worldwide brands are SAP, Baan, Oracle, J.D. Edwards, PeopleSoft, and the like. Apart from these, we can also see specialized brands like Algorithm, Reteck, and JDA, which cater to the specific industries.

One has to clearly understand here that ERP is *not* SAP, or Baan or anything else, but these are the tools of ERP. The concepts that ERP believes in ideally should get reflected in these products. But we see that not everything is observed in the same way because of many reasons, primarily attributed to **marketing strategy.**

Every ERP company offers its brand with different marketing strategies. Hence we find significant differences in ***procedures, forms, looks, nomenclatures, reporting structures, facilities, architecture, database designs, and also the prices*** for different ERP products. Since these products vary in their functional and technical efficiencies, it is crucial for the client side to decide which product to opt for huge investment. Of course, most of these products are based on common theory but ***different implementation experience at their (gin pig) clients.*** They are evolved from the state of small automation and planning software that was addressing a particular business process. Thus we find that the strengths of these products are different in addressing various business processes. For example, one popular ERP brand is evolved from *inventory management system*. Hence we find it very strong in all materials transaction functionalities. Another brand is evolved from *maintenance management system,* which handles maintenance planning in a unique way with excellent efficiency. One brand is evolved from highly focused area of *human resource management.* Thus we find different strengths and weaknesses of these products. Let us now discuss these products in detail.

SAP

Founded in 1972 in Waldorf, Germany, SAP AG (Systems, Applications and Products in Data Processing) is a leading global provider of client/server business application solutions [SAP]. Most prominent among SAP's product range are the enterprise application suites R/2 and R/3: R/2 applications for the mainframe environment and the more recent R/3 applications for open client/server applications. With both R/2 and R/3, SAP customers can choose to install the core system and one or more of the component sub-systems, or purchase the software as a complete package.

With over 1000 business processes and applications built into the software, SAP R/3 can integrate a company's entire organization. A company's business information is shared real-time with employees, suppliers and distributors—whether the company has 50 employees or 100,000. SAP's R/3 (and R/2) applications are composed of several tightly integrated components called *modules*. Some of the more common SAP R/3 modules are:

FI (Financial Accounting): Collects all corporate data relevant to accounting, providing complete documentation and up-to-the minute information for enterprise-wide control and planning.

CO (Control): Compatible planning and control instruments for company-wide controlling systems, with a uniform reporting system for coordinating contents and procedures of a company's internal processes.

PP (Product Planning): Provides comprehensive processes for all types of manufacturing, from repetitive, make-to-order, through process, lot and make-to-stock manufacturing, to integrated supply chain management.

MM (Materials Management): Optimizes all purchasing processes with work-flow driven processing functions, enabling automated supplier evaluation, lowering procurement and warehousing costs with accurate inventory and warehouse management.

SD (Sales and Distribution): Supports sales and distribution activities with outstanding functions for pricing, prompt order processing, on-time delivery, and interactive multilevel variant configuration.

HR (Human Resources Management): Provides solutions for planning and managing a company's human resources, simplifying personnel management tasks.

SAP Industry Solutions

SAP industry solutions offer in-depth functionality for 21 business groups, building on the powerful functions and comprehensive capabilities of our cross-industry solutions. These solutions fall under the following two categories: Manufacturing and Service as shown in Table 4.1(a).

Table 4.1(a) SAP Industry Solutions: Categories

Manufacturing	Service
Aerospace and Defense	Banking
Automotive	Financial Service Providers
Chemicals	Healthcare
Consumer Products	Higher Education and Research
Engineering and Construction	Insurance
High Tech	Media
Mill Products	Public Sector
Mining	Retail
Oil and Gas	Service Providers
Pharmaceuticals	Telecommunications

The SAP implementation in India is as given in Table 4.1(b).

Table 4.1(b) SAP Implementation in India

ABB	Asian Paints
Alcatel Modi	Arvind Mills
BPCL	Bharat Forge
TELCO	Colour Chem.
Cadbury India	Crompton Greaves
Colgate Palmolive India	DCM Shriram
TISCO	IOC
Du Pont India	Essar Oil
Eicher Goodearth	Marico Industries
General Motors India	Grasim
Hoechst	Haldia Petrochemicals
JCT Electronics	Indian Rayon
Mercedes-Benz India	Ispat Industries
Modi Telstra	Kalyani Brakes
Proctor & Gamble India	L & T
Samsung India	Mahindra & Mahindra
Siemens	Malayala Manorama
Volvo India	MICO
Ranbaxy	Microland
Times of India	ONGC

ORACLE

Oracle, the world's second-largest software company, has an enterprise package solution in almost all business areas: the Oracle Applications include Oracle Financials, Oracle Manufacturing, Oracle HRMS (payroll, personnel), and Oracle

Supply Chain Management. More than 4000 customers in over 60 countries worldwide use Oracle applications. Oracle's revenue from applications software licenses and application-related services is growing rapidly.

Among these business areas, Oracle has the resources to develop a product that could be a significant player in the financial area. Oracle Financials is a full-function financial management and accounting solution that includes: general ledger, fixed assets, order entry, accounts payable, purchasing, accounts receivable, inventory revenue accounting, and project accounting. Oracle also provides solutions for the financial services industry, which allows customers to access any financial product or services at any time from anywhere. At the same time, it provides executives and account managers with immediate access to the critical information they need.

Oracle e-Business Suite is a complete set of business applications that enables you to efficiently manage customer interactions, deliver services, manufacture products, ship orders, collect payments and more—all from a system built on a unified information architecture._The various functional modules under e-business suit are:

- Manufacturing
- Marketing
- Order Management
- Procurement
- Projects
- Sales
- Service
- Contracts
- Financials
- Human Resources
- Learning Management
- Maintenance Management

Oracle Industry Specific Solutions

Oracle's industry specific solutions are as shown:

- Aerospace and Defense
- Automotive
- Chemicals
- Communications
- Consumer Packaged Goods
- Energy
- Engineering and Construction

- Financial Services
- Government
- Healthcare
- High Technology
- Higher Education
- Industrial Manufacturing
- Life Sciences
- Professional Services
- Retail
- Travel and Transportation
- Utilities

Oracle Implementations in India

Kellogs India Limited	Spice Telecom, Bangalore
Motorola (p) Limited	Sona Steering
Synthetics and Chemicals	BPL Uptron Picture Tube
DLF Universal Limited	HCl GI
Great Eastern Shipping Co. Ltd.	GE Silicon
GE	Surat Electricity Board
Andhra Pradesh Rayon	Kirloskar Oil Engines
Punj Lloyd Ltd.	Dishergarh Power Supply
Indian Aluminium Co. Ltd.	Adani Ports
Asahi India Safety Glass Ltd.	Usha Martin Telecom
Gontermann Peipers India	Wipro Limited- ESD
Birla AT&T	L&T – ECC
BPL US West	BPL Ltd. – CMO
Lanka Bell	FACIL
Sony India Pvt. Ltd.	Jindal Vijaynagar Steel Ltd.
Maruti Udyog Ltd.	Stone India Ltd.
Bharti Cellular Ltd.	Culcutta Electricity Supply Corporation

PEOPLESOFT

PeopleSoft Inc. was founded by Dave Duffield and Ken Morris in 1987, when they built the first human resources application on a client-server platform instead of the traditional mainframe, adding needed flexibility and putting more power into the hands of users. Today, PeopleSoft employs more than 8000 employees worldwide, has more than 3000 customers in 144 countries generating annual revenue of 1.8 billion.

PeopleSoft develops markets and supports enterprise-wide software solutions to handle core business functions including Human Resource Management, Accounting and Control, Project Management, Treasury Management, Performance Measurement, and Supply Chain Management.

Extremely renowned for its customer service PeopleSoft, dedicates approximately 47 per cent of its staff to customer service in the areas of accounts management, product support, professional services, educational services and communication services.

PeopleSoft began its operation with a human resource management system that automated one of the most labour- and time-intensive functions of any business and client/server technology. It is the main competitor of SAP in the human resource and payroll area. PeopleSoft is one of America's fastest growing companies.

Industry Solutions

PeopleSoft industry solutions leverage best practices and industry domain expertise to deliver the best fit for the specific company's needs. It delivers specific solutions for every industry as it has its own requirements—whether they are regulatory, feature functionality, industry-specific products or complete solutions. The Industry verticals catered to by PeopleSoft are:

- Banking and Capital Markets
- Communications
- Public Sector
- Wholesale Distribution
- Staffing
- Professional Service Organizations
- Insurance
- Higher Education
- High Technology
- Healthcare
- Consumer Products

One of the features of PeopleSoft is that it focuses on medium-sized companies. Its packaged software *PeopleSoft Select* offers solutions that simplify the application selection and implementation process on Microsoft NT and SQL Server platforms.

BAAN

Baan is a business application and consulting company whose headquarters is in the Netherlands and California. It delivers comprehensive enterprise-wide business management software to companies worldwide requiring best-in-class manufacturing capabilities. BMCS (Baan Manufacturing Control System) was the first package developed by Baan for MRP-I, CRP and MRP-II.

More than 4000 companies use Baan in 5000 sites worldwide. Baan conducts manufacturing, finance, distribution, and service and maintenance operations. Baan applications support multiple currency, language, and taxation features.

Product Functionality

The company's flagship product, Baan IV, is a suite of open-systems-based, software applications for enterprise information management. The software enables companies to manage all aspects of the business; from sales forecasting and inventory control, to manufacturing, distribution, and finance in one, integrated environment.

Baan is enabling a new paradigm called *Dynamic Enterprise Modelling*, which delivers a framework for ensuring that enterprise applications are in close alignment with an organization's changing processes and business model.

While supporting finance, sales, purchasing, logistics and service functions, its major strength, lies in the **manufacturing** modules that allow discrete manufacturers to do what they do best—whether your core process is make-to-stock, make-to-order, engineer-to-order, configure-to-order, assemble-to-order, or all of these at the same time.

Baan IV is specially designed to meet the needs of key vertical markets such as automotive, electronics, heavy equipment and contract manufacturing, specialty chemicals, and food and beverage. It supports the entire spectrum of a company's critical business processes. Baan ERP includes the following components:

- Baan Manufacturing
- Baan Project
- Baan Finance
- Baan Service
- Baan Process
- Baan Distribution and Transportation

Baan Industry Specific Solutions

- Aerospace and Defense
- Automotive
- Equipment and Machinery
- Process Manufacturing
- Logistics

Baan Implementations in India

Calcom India	Advanced Tech Devices
Alstom	Bharat Bijilee
Indo-Asian Group	Blue Star
New Holland Tractors	Eimco Elecon
Rallis India	Elgi Equipment
Samsonite India	Ennore Foundries
Sony India	Forbes and Walker
Sulzer Pumps	Godrej & Boyce
Tata IBM	Sundaram Clayton
Vam Organics	Jay Bharat Maruti
Thermax	Metastrips
Vulcan	L & T
Unichem	Media Tel

J.D. EDWARDS

Founded in 1977 by Jack Thomson, Dan Gregory, and Ed McVaney and headquartered in Denver (Colorado), J.D. Edwards focuses on long-term business partnerships helping its 6700 customers in more than 110 countries. The company—through electronic medium—collaborates with its customers business to manage their business processes, supply chains, enterprise assets, and supplier and customer relationships. J.D. Edwards makes customers stronger, enabling them to solve their most important business challenges. The company offers collaborative enterprise software as well as consulting, education and support services. These offerings are differentiated by a deeply ingrained attitude of listening to customers, innovating on their behalf, and delivering solutions as part of a result-oriented relationship. It is a leading provider of Idea to Action enterprise applications, encompassing flexible, integrated software for distribution, finance, human resources, manufacturing and supply chain management.

Products

In the 1980s, J.D. Edwards was the leading supplier of applications software for the highly successful IBM AS/400 computer with their product **WorldSoftware**. In 1996, **OneWorld** was introduced, which combined a full range of platform independent applications with an integrated toolset. J.D. Edwards offers its solution primarily for the AS/400 platform. J.D. Edward's two application suites, OneWorld and World Software/**WorldVision**, provide comprehensive supply chain management functionality across the technology continuum, from host centric, to thin client, to network centric computing. All three can run concurrently on the same AS/400, share data, and interact with each other as a unified solution. OneWorld is flexible enough to support an extended solution by integrating with the Legacy System. It embraces change with its modular architectural foundation. The information processing is segmented into five functional elements, namely, database, data warehouse, data objects, reporting, and GUI. The users can link these elements in a variety of configurations ranging from one tier, with every element running on a standalone PC, to five tiers or more.

In OneWorld, one can distribute the enterprise applications to employees, business partners and customers using web based technology, without rewriting the applications. This results in an extended enterprise that works together to support the same business tasks.

OneWorld has an architecture neutral foundation that mediates between the business solution and technical underpinning. That allows it to accommodate a full suite of databases (including DB2, SQL Server and Oracle) and Hardware Technologies.

OneWorld's toolset uses business logic, and not symbols or syntax to drive the modifications and alterations to make the applications fit precisely as per the organizational requirements. As the business specifications change, the toolset automatically generates the appropriate object code. Application modification balancing processing loads; running reports and graphical user interfaces may be built without writing codes. Hardware and databases may be added without bringing the business to a halt.

The different product modules available from J.D. Edwards are:

- Foundation Suite
- Financial Suite
- Logistics/Distribution Suite
- Services Suite
- Manufacturing Suite
- Architecture, Engineering, Construction, Mining and Real Estate Suite
- Energy and Chemical Suite
- Payroll Suite
- Human Resources Suite
- Customer Services Management Suite
- Government, Education and Not-for-Profit Solutions
- Utility and Energy Solutions

J.D. Edwards Industry Specific Solutions

- Automotive
- Chemicals
- Construction
- Consumer Products
- Energy
- Field Service

- Financial Services
- High Tech/Electronics, Homebuilders
- Industrial Manufacturing
- Life Sciences
- Mining
- Professional Services
- Public Services
- Paper
- Real Estate Telecommunications

RAMCO

Ramco Systems was founded in 1989 by P.R. Ramasubrahmaneya Rajha with expertise in Enterprise Solutions and Services, Custom Solutions, CRM, Networking and Information Security.

More than 1200 IT professionals of Ramco Systems operating in 15 offices across seven countries are engaged in R&D, Application Research, Development and Implementation to serve 1000 customer installations worldwide. Ramco Systems provides multiple options for solution engagement as required by the needs of the customer. Specific choice of the engagement model can be decided once the project scope boundaries are finalized.

The main product of the company is branded as **Ramco Marshall,** which provides a unique approach featuring distributed computing, breadth of applications, and flexibility. It divides the processing load between the client and the server. Application logic that does not require any external data, and the graphical user interface are placed on the client.

Marshall consists of 35 applications in nine functional areas namely,

1. Process Production
2. Discrete Production
3. Sales
4. Treasury
5. Financials
6. Human Resources
7. Logistics
8. Plant Maintenance
9. Statistical Process and Quality Control.

Each application module is capable of working alone or with other Marshall or third party applications in any configuration, in order to meet specific business needs.

Ramco Implementations in India

- Addisons & Co Ltd.
- Aditya Cement

- Amtrex
- Bakelite Hylam Ltd.
- BEML
- Cadila Pharmaceuticals
- Carborundum Universal
- Coats India
- Parry's Confectionery Ltd.
- Dr. Reddy's Lab.
- Escotel Mobile Communications Ltd.
- FOSROC Chemicals
- Ghrada Chemicals Ltd.
- GTL
- HDFC Bank
- Hutchison Max
- Jindal Iron and Steel Ltd.
- Madura International Textiles
- Indian Aluminium Company Ltd.
- JCT Ltd.

QAD

QAD was founded in 1979 and now has its presence in 21 countries. The company's major product offerings include MFG/PRO, ON/Q, Service/Support Management, Decision support, and Qwizard.

The company's flagship product is its ERP solution branded as *MFG/PRO*. It is available in 26 languages and has more than 4000 installed sites.

Products

QAD offers a variety of Supply Chain and ERP software products to manufacturing industries within the automotive, consumer products, electronics, industrial products and medicine sector.

MFG/PRO software provides, along with it, an integrated Global Supply Chain Management solution that includes manufacturing, distribution, financial and support management application within an open system environment. It is claimed to be one of the most successful Client/Server ERP applications as it dramatically increases the internal efficiencies of distributed operations within months of purchase.

The software is comprehensive, open, flexible, scalable, and interactive and is designed to address the operations requirements of the industries.

MFG/PRO uses either Oracle or progress database, and runs in UNIX, Windows and Windows NT. It is available with a GUI or character user interface.

MFG/PRO's supply function includes centralized order processing, centralized purchasing, enterprise operations planning, and enterprise material transfer. It addresses the entire manufacturing spectrum from repetitive to configure-to-order and batch process to make-to-stock. With this system, one can manage supplies within the enterprise more effectively, no matter how widely distributed the sites are.

The various Modules in MFG/PRO are:

Distribution: This module of MFG/PRO is used to monitor inventory balances and purchasing and sales order activities.

Manufacturing: This Manufacturing module of MFG/PRO is to regulate all manufacturing activities within various types of production environments.

Financials: The financial module interface with the Distribution, Manufacturing planning modules to asses the financial implications of the company's activities.

Services/Support: This module is designed for companies while not only manufacture and sell their products but also provide after sales services and support.

Supply/Chain: This module is for the control of goods and information from supplier to customer.

Master files: Master file function provides access to a series of foundation modules that are used by the rest of the MFG/PRO applications. These master files include Item/Sites, Address/Taxes, Inventory control settings, physical inventory, multiple databases, and managerial functions.

ERP DOMAIN EXPERTISE

We have seen above the popular brands of ERP and their claims. It is now interesting to analyze the strengths of these brands in various functional domains.

Oracle Financials

Oracle Financials is a full-function financial management and accounting solution that includes general ledger, fixed assets, order entry, accounts payable, purchasing, accounts receivable, inventory revenue accounting, and project accounting. Oracle also provides solutions for the financial services industry, which allows customers to access any financial product or services at any time from anywhere. At the same time, it provides executives and account managers with immediate access to the critical information they need. The major components of Oracle financials package are now described.

Activity based management: Oracle Activity Based Management offers the ability to create, analyze, and monitor activity based management information from pilot projects to enterprise wide implementations. This system provides accurate cost information to help managers throughout the organization to improve profitability and resource allocation at any level. Going beyond traditional cost allocation, Activity Based Management models the complexity of all costs based on activities, materials, resources, and product and service components.

Assets: Oracle Assets is a comprehensive asset management solution that streamlines the tracking, depreciation and maintenance scheduling of assets. Oracle Assets is part of the Oracle e-Business Suite, an integrated set of applications that offer complete process automation and full information.

Balanced scorecard: Oracle Balanced Scorecard enables the true linkage of strategy to management actions by placing the company's Key Performance Indicators (KPIs) on managers' desktops, and giving them direct and quantifiable targets to achieve. By illustrating the cause and effect relationships between KPIs, the Oracle Balanced Scorecard gives managers a clear understanding of how their decisions impact both their direct area of responsibility and the overall company strategy. The Oracle Balanced Scorecard is used across all industries, including manufacturing, service, public sector, and non-profit organizations.

Cash management: Oracle Cash Management is an enterprise-wide solution for managing liquidity and controlling cash. With Oracle Cash Management, it is possible to have project cash flows based on source data from the Oracle e-Business Suite and external systems.

Collections: Oracle Collections provides detailed information on delinquent customers, payments, disputes, and promises to pay. This helps users to quickly identify delinquent customers and employ proactive contact methods to obtain payment. Oracle Collections is an integral area of Oracle Revenue and Receivables Management, a set of applications within Oracle Financials designed to help companies ensure revenue recognition integrity, to confidently predict cash flows, and effectively minimize the risk of financial misstatement.

Credit management: Oracle Credit Management empowers the credit manager to continually monitor and evaluate the creditworthiness of customers and prospects. Using Oracle Credit Management, companies can accept credit applications, analyze them and make credit award decisions. Oracle Credit Management offers out-of-the-box integration with third party credit information that sources to ensure the best possible decisions are made. Oracle Credit Management is an integral area of Oracle Revenue and Receivables Management, a set of applications within Oracle Financials designed to help companies ensure revenue recognition integrity, confidently predict cash flows, and effectively minimize the risk of financial misstatement.

Financials and sales analyzer: Oracle Financial Analyzer enables to quickly analyze performance, develop new plans, and easily revise budgets and forecasts. Users can employ these applications to develop and analyze performance metrics, evaluate risks and plan future direction since good sales and marketing professionals use Oracle Sales Analyzer to identify new opportunities, measure promotional effectiveness, track product sales, and forecast future results.

General ledger: Oracle General Ledger enables to institute statutory financial controls, reduce the period close cycle, access financial data, and deliver comprehensive financial reporting. It is the fastest and most scaleable accounting solution on the market and supports the highest transaction rates, largest data volumes, and smallest processing windows.

Global consolidation system: Oracle Global Consolidation System, a multi-source financial consolidation tool, provides strong financial controls and strategic financial information, shorten the consolidation process, provide accurate, timely, consolidated financial data, and reduce administrative costs.

Oracle internal controls manager: Oracle Internal Controls Manager is a comprehensive tool that enables one to document and test internal controls and monitor ongoing compliance. It helps users comply with all the legal regulations as well as mitigate operational risk, reduce the likelihood of financial misstatement, safeguard corporate assets, and improve operational efficiency.

Internet expenses: Oracle Internet Expenses is a self-service application that enables employees to submit, approve and manage their expenses online, leading to reduction in transaction processing costs, reimbursement cycle times, data errors, as well as improving the employee productivity. It supports multi-currency transactions, global tax requirements, charge card statement download, and charge card direct payment.

Payables: Oracle Payables is an expenditure management application that streamlines the procure-to-pay process while providing strong financial controls and strategic financial information. It enables one to receive and pay invoices automatically, ensure the necessary controls over disbursements, and optimize cash management.

Property manager: Oracle Property Manager is the cornerstone of the Oracle e-Business Suite's real estate offering. Its ability to support lease execution from both the tenant's and the landlord's perspective addresses the needs of corporate real estate management, commercial property management, retail/franchise operations, and real estate investment trusts (REITs). Along with Oracle Projects and Oracle Enterprise Asset Management, Oracle Property Manager simplifies the complexity of real estate management through integration with the rest of the Oracle e-Business Suite.

Receivables: Oracle Receivables is an invoicing and collections management application that efficiently streamlines the order-to-cash process while providing strong financial controls and strategic financial information. Oracle Receivables is the cornerstone of Oracle Revenue and Receivables Management, a set of applications within Oracle Financials designed to help companies ensure revenue recognition integrity, confidently predict cash flows, and effectively minimize the risk of financial misstatement.

Revenue and receivables management: Oracle Revenue and Receivables Management is a comprehensive, integrated solution that improves cash flow, increases efficiencies, and enforces strong corporate discipline. By streamlining the delinquency, deduction, and dispute management processes, collections intelligence feedsback into the credit decision process, along with external information.

Treasury: Oracle Treasury is an integrated solution for managing corporate treasury operations with improved efficiency, profitability and control. It is an integrated part of the Oracle e-Business Suite, which offers complete process automation and complete information.

mySAP ERP

SAP's Enterprise Resource Planning (ERP) solution, mySAP ERP, has been designed to provide a comprehensive solution to today's changing demands on ERP. While leveraging existing IT assets, mySAP ERP allows companies to regain active control of their whole administrative and operations environment and thereby increase efficiency and profitability. mySAP ERP enables new levels of business process and technology integration while laying the foundation for incremental evolution. In the past, ERP systems were wholly designed with an internal backend business focus. However, an increasing number of companies are beginning to realize the need for efficiency in the administrative and operative environment that today extends to almost every employee's desktop. Therefore, there is a growing requirement for expandable ERP solutions which will allow companies to collaborate and extend their ERP processes. mySAP serves these requirements with its various key functional modules discussed now.

Strategic enterprise management: This enables companies to execute strategies quickly and successfully while managing business performance throughout the organization; supports integrated strategic planning, performance monitoring, business consolidation, and effective stakeholder communication, thus enabling value-based management.

Business analytics: Allows managers and knowledge workers within an integrated framework to identify and exploit value-adding opportunities within the daily business-enabling optimization of operational performance, accurate forecasting, and business planning; identifies opportunities to create additional value through better exploitation of tangible and intangible assets, such as customer value, human capital, or the R&D pipeline value.

Financial accounting: It helps companies to not only monitor real-time values from financially relevant transactions out of value-creation processes but also to maintain a consistent, reconciled, and auditable set of books for statutory reporting, management support, and as a source for analytic applications.

Managerial accounting: Helps companies optimally monitor and control all performance relevant information in an environment that is completely integrated with all operative transactions throughout the company.

Manager self-service: Provides business managers with access to all relevant business information as well as related services through financial portal solutions. Additionally, this capability helps manage financially shared service centres. Content and application services facilitate better, faster decision making and increased productivity through manager-centric portals. HR content and processes empower anyone who manages and makes decisions about finance, management and human capital.

Employee transaction management: Streamlines a comprehensive range of HR services and processes necessary to efficiently run the Human Resource environment. This includes a global system meeting the needs of local regulatory compliance requirements as well as international best practices.

Employee lifecycle management: Provides automation and optimization of the following phases of the employee life cycle-attract/hire, deploy, influence, develop, and retain resulting in increased human capital efficiency through better hiring practices, more efficient deployment, focused employee development, and increased employee retention and loyalty.

E-recruiting: Helps locate the best people and coordinate team collaboration to identify and evaluate candidates. Some elements are talent warehouse, recruiter, service centre, and analytics. Advanced portal and collaboration technology enable the solution to allow efficient collaboration between business partners.

Employee relationship management: Provides companies with the ability to enable employees throughout the company to build collaborative relationships with fellow employees, managers, third-party suppliers, and the company itself. Knowledge management and portal technology are utilized to significantly change the HR service delivery model and efficiency of the workforce.

Employee self-service: Content and application services offer a multitude of ready-to-use individual ESS services available in 32 languages for 32 countries, giving employees control over multiple administrative tasks. With life-and-work events capabilities, individual transactions are seamlessly combined with expert content and knowledge so that the employee experience is efficient and enjoyable.

HCM analytics: Provides data analysis and reporting tools as well as strategic enterprise management capabilities to support informed HR policy and decision-making. The solutions enable the company to analyze and optimize the current workforce, to implement and monitor the corporate strategy, and to continuously evaluate how different scenarios will affect business goals.

Purchase order management: Enables the efficient handling and execution of Purchase Orders integrated within the entire logistics process.

Inventory management: Allows a company an integrated management of stock and inventories in an integrated operative environment.

Production management: Enables the efficient management and execution of the entire production process.

Maintenance and quality: Allows a company to efficiently handle the plant maintenance and quality control process within the company.

Delivery management: Executes the delivery and transportation processes to efficiently support a sales environment.

Sales order management: Enables the sales order fulfillment process allowing for fast and efficient execution of customer sales orders.

Baan Manufacturing

The Baan Software is a group of integrated enterprise resource planning tools that take advantage of all the actual technologies and business principles in the market world. Its strength is in **Manufacturing** function, which is supported by tools such as Business Organizer to ensure quick implementation of product as well as a proper fit to the customer's process.

The Manufacturing Module of Baan is designed to control all the operations related to products fabrication, labour management and capacity required, while planning functions such as Master Production Schedule, Material Requirements Planning, and Capacity Planning complement this module. Baan offers various options for planning and control of the manufacturing activities within an organization. It has powerful capabilities that address all the manufacturing environments, such as make-to-stock, make-to-order, assemble-to-order and engineer-to-order.

Baan manufacturing can handle these situations in a seamless manner and is ideal for industries working in multiple environments. It has the following major functional modules.

Bill of Material: The Bill of Material Control Module helps maintain the product structure of the manufactured product describing the parent-child relationships between the items.

Routing: Routing can be described as a path taken by an item during the course of its manufacture. The various stages and the time periods are recorded in the routing module.

Master Production Schedule (MPS): Master Production Schedule represents apex level plan of Baan MRP II. This plan is composed of the following three subplans:

- Demand Plan
- Production Plan
- Inventory Plan

The Master Production Schedule module allows creating different scenarios for these plans and comparing them.

Materials Requirement Planning (MRP): MRP logic in Baan can run in three ways:

- Regenerative MRP
- Net Change MRP
- Continuous MRP

Complete MRP run is carried out in regenerative type without considering the previous MRP calculations. Only changes of MPS and MRP items with respect to the previous run are calculated in net change MRP which requires a lesser duration than the regenerative MRP run. Continuous MRP is basically a net change MRP run that runs itself after a definite time period.

Capacity Requirement Planning (CRP): CRP module is designed to give the planner an insight into the use of work centres and machines based on the planning carried out. In principle, the required capacity is planned on the basis of infinite capacity. However, various reports and displays in this module highlight the projected bottlenecks.

Shop floor control: Having accomplished the planning at the MPS, MRP and CRP level, the next step is to monitor and report the operations at the shop floor level.

Baan Manufacturing module also offers facilities to perform financial analysis where it can reflect the projected profitability.

Apart from these major functions, Baan Manufacturing module has the following business objects:

- Engineering Data Management
- Item Control
- Repetitive Manufacturing
- Hours Accounting
- Project Budget
- Product Configuration
- Product Classification
- Project Control
- Quality Management System

PeopleSoft Human Capital Management

PeopleSoft Human Capital Management solutions include:

- HRMS
- Workforce Analytics
- Sales Incentive Management
- Enterprise Learning Solutions

Human Resources Management (HRM): PeopleSoft 8 HRMS lets the enterprise manage HR business processes from recruitment to retirement with pure Internet applications which are built on a best-practices performance record of more than 10 years. With PeopleSoft HRMS, a company can extend the reach of the organization by pulling external content into our suite of employee and manager self-service applications, all of which are delivered through a role-base portal. It helps align the workforce with strategic business goals with analytics for better, faster decision-making.

The company claims that nine out of the top 10 Fortune 500 companies, including Exxon-Mobil, Wal-Mart, General Motors, Ford, Citigroup, IBM, AT&T, and Verizon Communications use PeopleSoft HRMS applications.

Workforce analytics: PeopleSoft Workforce Analytics provides the tools to measure, manage, and maximize the workforce performance.

HRMS warehouse: Manage the workforce information for analytic reporting and analysis.

Workforce planning: Align the workforce competencies with organizational goals.

Workforce rewards: Plan compensation and retention initiatives.

Workforce scorecard: Assess the impact of the workforce on enterprise operations to determine how best to meet future business objectives.

Sales Incentive Management (SIM): Enables organizations to influence and reward sales force behaviour. It offers a portfolio of features to support the entire sales incentive management process. It is the first product to be released within the Enterprise Incentive Management suite of applications and is now available as part of PeopleSoft's industry-leading Human Capital Management (HCM) suite.

Enterprise learning solutions: PeopleSoft Enterprise Learning is a pure Internet solution that empowers enterprises to provide the right learning to the right people, at the right time, in the right format. With PeopleSoft Enterprise Learning Solutions, an organization can approach learning strategically. It helps improve enterprise performance by planning and deploying learning within and beyond the enterprise to customers, suppliers, and employees. By using Enterprise Learning Solutions, companies can integrate learning across all business processes, provide intelligent learning advice to the workforce, customers, and suppliers, and can align learning with corporate objectives.

SUMMARY

We have discussed in this chapter various ERP brands and their suitability to various industry sectors. Table 4.2 shows the summarized views on ERP brands. The analysis made in the table is indicative and the changes are taking place at a very fast pace. One has to get updated every moment to get the current picture.

Table 4.1 Comparative Analysis of Major ERP Vendors

Criteria \ Company	SAP	Oracle	PeopleSoft	Baan	Ramco Systems	J.D. Edwards	QAD
Year of establisment	1972	1977	1987	1978	1989	1977	1979
Country	Germany	USA	USA	Netherlands	India	USA	USA
Flagship product	R/3	Oracle Application	PeopleSoft 8	Baan IV	Marshall	OneWorld	MFG/PRO
Strength area	Presence across all functions & industry verticals	Financials	Human capital management	Manufacturing	Cost/Speed of Deployment	Construction/ Energy & utilities	Distribution & Discrete manufacturing
Latest offering	mySAP SCM/ CRM/PLM	Oracle 11i e-business suit	AppConnect	iBaan	Virtual works & e.applications	WorldSoftware	MFG/PRO eb2
Development tool	ABAP/4	Oracle forms	Peopletools	BaanC	—	J.D.P. ower tools	—
Comprehensive & industry specific	Yes	Yes	No	No	No	Yes	No
Major implementations	High end & mid-market	High end & mid-market	High end market	High end & mid-market	Mid-market & SMEs	Mid-market	Mid-market

EXERCISES

1. What is the difference between ERP and tools for ERP? Why any ERP brand cannot be regarded as the complete ERP solution?
2. How is SAP's marketing strategy different from Baan in India?
3. Enlist various modules available in Oracle Financials and JD Edwards' Oneworld?
4. "Strength of ERP brand depends upon its past implementation experience." Discuss with examples and cases.
5. Compare the advantages of Oracle manufacturing against Baan with reference to Semiconductor manufacturing (Hi-tech) industrial sector.

CHAPTER 5 Basic Functional Modules in ERP

The basic functional requirements of any process-based manufacturing organization in ERP context can be classified as follows:

Manufacturing Requirements

In this all the manufacturing related data sets have to be modelled and proper information should be created to facilitate efficient and economic production. Typically, it may include information regarding items, bill of materials, routings, formula (in case of process industries), machines, instruments, master production scheduling, material and capacity requirement planning, quality management, etc.

Distribution Requirements

The word "distribution" has to be properly interpreted in the ERP context. It means "related to materials". Hence we can include procedures for functionalities like purchasing, selling, inventory, DRP (Distribution Requirement Planning), replenishments, lot controlling, location related formalities, etc.

Financial Requirements

In this area we may include working capital issues, long-term investment planning, accounts payables and receivables, cash balancing, voucher maintenance, treasury, trial balancing, profit–loss measurements, presentations, etc.

It is expected that ERP products should offer proper and user-friendly options for all these requirements in terms of various ***functional modules***. We have seen in Chapter 4 that some ERP products are slightly different from each other, whereas some other ERP products are significantly different from each other in their capabilities to address various business requirements. Still, they have a common theme. We will now discuss a few of the ERP modules that help users to function in a world class environment.

ITEM CONTROL MODULE IN ERP

Item can be defined in ERP context as any entity, tangible or intangible, with which a cost is associated. In a simpler way, we can say anything which has a cost associated with it and is not an asset, is an item. Items can be classified into six generic types as shown in Figure 5.1.

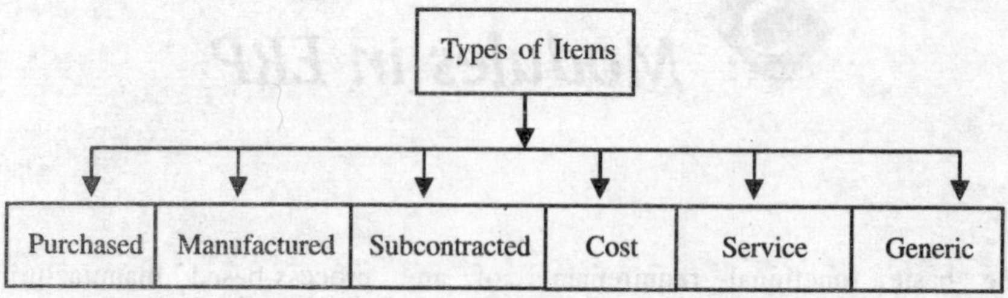

Figure 5.1 Item types in ERP.

1. Purchased item: Any item purchased from outside is termed as a *purchased item*. These items include raw materials, packing materials, etc.

2. Manufactured item: Any item manufactured within an organization is termed as a *manufactured item*. These items include assemblies, production items, etc..

3. Subcontracted items: An item that is directly sent to the customers from the sub-contractors is termed as a *subcontracted item*. These items include third party manufactured items.

4. Cost items: Cost items are consumption items for which no inventory is maintained. These items include electricity, some spare parts, consumables, etc.

5. Service items: Any service, which is either consumed or provided comes under this classification. These items include AMC (Annual Maintenance Contract), and other related items.

6. Generic item: This is a configurable item. These items include configurable assemblies, transmission systems, motors, etc.

The item control module is the cornerstone for integration of various ERP packages at the functional level. Item control module is divided into sections of similar information. These sections can be defined depending on the type of information. The data required by item control module are as follows:

- General and cost price data
- Inventory data
- Purchase and sales data
- Order data
- Production/Manufacturing/Assembling data

The objective of entering this data is to maintain standard item data, which will be used throughout the ERP packages. About 150 data fields are required to be populated into ERP package so as to generate one new item. Some ERP packages like Baan also provide the facility to accommodate customized item data apart from standard item data. In item control, the real requirement is to devote more "front end" time to developing and loading quality data and well-defined parameters, rather than quickly loading this information and spending lots of the valuable time correcting and analyzing after the fact. We will now discuss various fields provided to describe an item.

General Data

Here the basic information of an item is loaded. The details of information are given in Table 5.1.

Table 5.1 General Fields of Item Control Module Confirm

Description	A field that accepts numbers as well as alphabets to describe item
Material	Material from which it is made
Size	Dimensions of an item
Weight	The mass or weight of field
Search key	The search keys are features that permit users to search for the item throughout the package
Item type	Item type places item in a pre-defined group of items (manufactured)
Item group	Item group enables one to define data for group of similar items
Selection	This information enables one to select the item by features such as history and statistical information
Signal code	The signal code causes a message to be displayed as soon as this item has been selected somewhere. It could also be used to block items through signal codes
Tax code	Tax applicable to item
Text	Whether any text is available about the item or not for reference.

This data has been entered primarily once for company's user community. Utilizing the search features, the user can navigate and search for the item throughout the system.

Inventory Data

Inventory data is utilized mainly by the distribution module and the material management module. Here units are assigned for storing goods; the warehouses are identified from where the goods will be transacted, item is determined whether it is lot controlled or not, and inventory plans are established. Table 5.2 shows the details of inventory data.

Table 5.2 Inventory Data Details

Units	Grouping of units for a specific application
Inventory unit	Unit used for costing
Storage unit	The storage unit is the unit in which items are stored
Warehouse	Warehouse for the item
Lot control	Whether item is lot controlled
Outbound priority	Outbound priority determines from which locations and lots the item is issued
Shelf life	Time unit for shelf life
Periods	No. of periods that item may be kept in stock
Service level	Service level determines how far the item can be delivered directly from stock
Safety stock	The amount of safety stock that serves as buffers to the uncertainties
Maximum inventory	Maximum inventory allowed
Seasonality	Seasonality is used to measure the safety stock to avoid capacity problems and forecasting demand
Forecast	Technique used for forecasting
Last inventory transaction date	This date tells when physical transaction for an item took place in warehouse
ABC code	Tells us about the importance of an item as per ABC costing
Inventory carrying cost	Percentage of dollar value of inventory per unit time

Purchase and Sales Data

The purchase and sales data will link the item master to obtain data on pricing and margin. This data helps the system for verification of purchase price, units that item will be stored in, the currency in which the item is purchased, etc. The system also develops the capability to refer, as a basis to sales price, suggested retail price, and the margin. Tables 5.3 and 5.4 give the details of all the information in purchase and sales data.

Table 5.3 Purchase Data

Purchase unit	The unit on which item is purchased
Price unit	The unit on which price is based
Price group	Group of items for which agreement about prices can be recorded
Currency	The currency is used when cost price is calculated
Purchase price	The purchase price of the item
Average purchase price	The price paid on an average
Latest price	The last price paid for last purchase
Supplier	The supplier from whom it is purchased
Buyer	Employee responsible for buying the item
Inspection	The field inspection determines the arrival procedure of purchased items

Table 5.4 Sales Data

Sale unit	Gather. The unit in which item is sold
Price unit	The unit on which selling price is based
Commission	Used to group when commission has to be paid
Group selling price	Used to define common rebate agreement
Recommended price	The selling price of item expressed in the currency
Upper margin	The upper margin is percentage of actual selling price above the target price
Last sales price	The sales price recommended by system to be charged to customer
Transaction date	The last date of changing SP

Order Data

The ordering details contain ordering data lead times, first allowed order date as well as minimum and maximum ordering quantities. This information would supply various other modules with the data that would permit accurate computation of material requirements. This data allows the system to assign the item to its proper ordering methodology. The system now applies the appropriate planning engine logic specified for this item for ordering purposes. These planning engines are master production schedule, materials requirement planning, or statistical inventory control. Table 5.5 gives the details of order data.

Table 5.5 Order Data Details

Order policy	The order policy defines how the item is controlled either anonymously or by the order.
Order method	The field is the mainly relevant item for items with the order method, "lot for lot", "EOQ".
Minimum order qty.	The minimum order quantity prevents the purchase or production of item in a smaller qty. than required.
Maximum order qty.	The maximum order qty. prevents the purchase or production of too many items for an order.
Reorder point	The reorder point is the average number of items, which are sold during the item's delivery time plus the safety stock.
Order interval	The order interval is the minimum required number of days between two orders of the same item.
Order lead time	The order lead-time is measured as how long the purchase or production of item lasts before it is available.
Safety time	An element of time added to normal lead-time to protect against uncertainty.

Production Data

The production data is required by item control to allow the user to identify the item as phantom or not and time fence associated with this item. The user can define the Bill of material and Routing units linked to this item as well as scrap factors and order costs. Table 5.6 provides the details of production data.

Table 5.6 Production Data Details

Phantom	An item is phantom when it appears in the product structure but is not seen as a separate manufactured item in production.
BoM	The BoM unit defines the number of manufactured items on which product structure is based.
Routing unit	The routing unit defines the information detailing the manufacture method of an item.
Shrink factor	A percent factor in BoM used to increase gross requirements to account for anticipated loss.
Order cost	Order costs are handling and transport costs as well as the costs of purchase and PPC departments, incurred for ordering.
Time fence	The time fence is a period in which changes only in planned production or purchased quantities for MPS items are possible.
Critical in MPS	Whether item is critical for the operation.
Low level code	A number that identifies the lowest level in any BoM at which the particular component appears.
Planner	The employee authorized for planning the item when it is to be purchased.
Pull note	Identifies the quantity to be released to shop floor.

Cost Price Information

The cost price information is the driver for calculation of the cost price of an item. A cost price calculation code is assigned to the item for calculation of cost price. Through this code user selects the purchase price to be considered, the current purchase, average price, latest purchase price, or a simulated price. Table 5.7 gives the details.

Table 5.7 Cost Price Information

Cost price component	The cost price component of the item to which the material costs is usually posted.
Standard cost price	The standard cost price is the sum of material and operation costs and cost price surcharges for the firm. The system shows what it costs to purchase or produce an item.
Material costs	Material costs are calculated by adding the cost of the materials and any surcharges that may have to be paid on the materials for the item under consideration.
Operations costs	Operation costs are calculated by adding the cost of the operations and any surcharges that have been paid for the operations for the item under consideration.
Last CP transaction date	The system shows the date on which the cost price of the item that was last changed. The last transaction date changes as soon as the cost price data is changed in the session Update Cost Prices.
Inventory valuation	The manner in which the stock for the item is valued.

We have seen above that various fields are needed to generate data about an item and then ERP will control the item in real time. The essence of item control is that no item is lying either as inventory (without any owner) or in a waiting queue. It can be said that the success of the ERP implementation greatly depends upon the way in which its Item Master is maintained and used. It demands world-class practices, for example, the supplier should dispatch the materials directly to the shop floor (if possible) so that storage is avoided, or as soon as the product is manufactured, it should be delivered instantly.

FORMULA MANAGEMENT/BoM MODULE OF ERP

Concept of Bill of Materials

The Bill of Material system provides for the maintenance and analysis of information regarding the structure of manufactured items. Maintenance is designed to be as efficient as possible, and a wide range of analysis reporting functions are provided. Inquiry displays and reports are generated dynamically at inquiry time so that the most current status of all pertinent inventory and product structure data is always available. Product structure maintenance is accomplished via a simple entry procedure, which requires the entry of first level components only. After entry of these single-level bills, the reporting functions have the ability to automatically explode all subassemblies, regardless of the number of levels of subassemblies and components involved.

Bill of Material Functions

- File maintenance functions
- Single-level parts list
- Phantom parts list
- Detailed parts list
- Summarized parts list
- Single-level usage list
- Phantom usage list
- Detailed usage list
- Summarized usage list
- Drawing cross-reference

The Bill of Material/Formula Management module provides the information required for real-time management of product/process structures and methods. It allows one to determine the precise material requirements and cost standards. This enables one to react to both anticipated and unanticipated events and schedule changes. We will now discuss the formula management module of ERP.

Concept of Formula Management

The basic idea of formula management is explained below:

1. It is used in process industries like pharmaceutical, chemical, cement, etc., where raw material consumption cannot be exactly estimated as in Bill of Material (BoM) consumption.
2. The main problem is the "actual" or "current" state of material (i.e. its pH value, potency, concentration, specific gravity, etc.) will decide the quantity to be used for making the product. For example, when one car is made, there is a 100% certainty that five tyres will be required. However, if one litre of chemical normally requires 500 ml of another chemical having 2.8 pH value, then at the time of manufacturing schedule, it may be observed that the required chemical has 3.8-pH value. Thus we may use 450 ml instead of 500 ml to achieve the same concentration of the finished goods. Thus it is expected that ERP systems facilitate these calculations. Figure 5.2 gives a pictorial description of formula management.

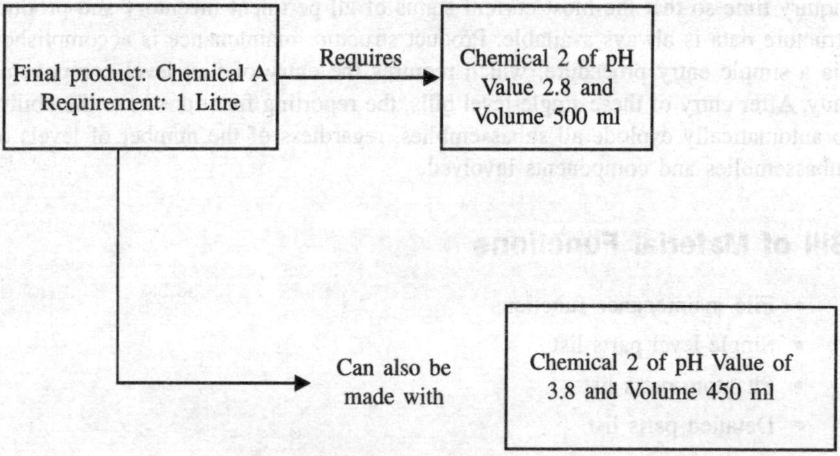

Figure 5.2 Illustration on formula management.

Baan Approach of Handling Formula Management

In the process industry, the product formula is the blueprint where information on ingredients, standard production quantities, and packaging configurations is used as a guideline for production. Chemical, pharmaceutical, food and beverage, metal companies and other sectors of the process industry combine these elements into a basis for product development, material requirements, production directives, and cost control activities.

Baan process formula and routing modules are designed to help one manage the information needed to manufacture process items. Discrete products are assembled from a set quantity of components included in a production bill of material. On the other hand, process manufactured goods are the outcome of a series of mixing operations, chemical reactions, extraction, and so on, which transform raw materials into a sellable product.

Part of the materials used in the formulation may get lost through evaporation, spillage, and so on. The processing of the ingredients can also yield goods other than the finished product; these can be reused, sold at a profit, or disposed of at a cost. In the same process, the processed good may go through other transformations where it is packaged in various types of containers and later inventoried as such.

Entering units of measure

- Baan enables one to determine whether process items are handled differently depending on how these are packaged.
- A company's standard unit of measure used to value inventory, establish formula quantities, and so forth must be linked to other units by means of a conversion factor. Baan supports six types of units of measure: weight, length, volume, piece, time, and area.
- After entering base units, additional units need to be entered, which are to be used for storage, valuation, and sales for the finished product, raw materials, and co-products.
- The next step followed is setting the conversion factors that ensure the proper conversion between the company's base unit and suppliers' and customers' units. Table 5.8 shows the complete procedure for accommodating conversion factor.

Table 5.8 Conversion Factor Fields

Base unit	If fields item and item groups are left blank, the base unit refers to the logistic company's base unit as set in the session Maintain Base Unit. If the conversion factor is set for a specific item or item group, the base unit refers to the product inventory unit.
Unit	The unit which is different from the company base unit or a product inventory unit for which one needs to set a conversion factor.
Conversion factor	The conversion factor between the base unit and the alternative unit.
Inverse value conversion factor	The conversion factor between the alternative and the base unit.
Power	If the conversion is between, for example, a unit representing a very small quantity and a unit representing a very large quantity, the conversion factor can be set with an exponential factor.

Creating unit sets: Unit sets are groups of units linked to various types of products. A unit set for raw materials may be different from that of finished goods, which may have more packaging configurations. Baan has two unit set codes: RAWMTL and FGOODS. For each of the units, one has to indicate whether they will be used as any of the following: Inventory units, distribution units, manufacturing units, price units, storage units and containers.

Entering process items in the item master: Before creating the formula for finished goods, the item master records for the raw materials, finished product and co/by-product need to be added to the item master. For example, consider the production of margarine: the item code MARG with the description-processed margarine can be entered. It also recommends defining the item as a manufactured, process item that is containerized.

Now, since the product is containerized, a conversion factor must be set between its base unit and the various packaging configurations tied to it. Also, the raw materials need to be entered as purchased, process items that are not containerized. For co-product Soya oil, which is assumed to be generated during the process and can be reused or sold, another product record has to be entered. The item is entered as manufactured, process item that is not containerized and its inventory unit has to be entered.

Creating a product formula in formula management module: The formula management module includes all sessions that pertain to product formulae such as maintain materials (mandatory), maintain end item containers (mandatory if the main item is containerized), and maintain co/by-products (optional). Two other sessions, maintain primary application and maintain product base, are used for various reporting or mass maintenance functions such as the session Replace Yield in Formula. Table 5.9 gives the formula details and Table 5.10 provides the detailed material fields.

Table 5.9 Maintain Formula Fields

Field name	Description
Formula item	The main item to be produced using the elements of the formula
Container	The container in which the formula item will be packaged. The field can be left blank if the formula being created is for the main item or the process item is not containerized (this is determined by the containerized field in the item master). If the process item is containerized, a formula for the end items must be created as well.
Formula size	The default quantity of the formula item to be produced.
Percentage formula	Identifies how the ingredients or materials of the formula must be entered. If this field is set to yes, some materials can be entered as percentages. If no, raw materials can only be entered as absolute quantities.
Formula type	Indicates whether the formula is ready for production or if it is in its test stage (model). Model formulae cannot be used in the production management module.
Yield percentage	It is the ratio of the usable output from a process to its input.
Effective date	The date in which the formula will become active. A production batch for this formula cannot be entered before this date.
Expiry date	The date on which the formula can no longer be used for production and has expired. If this field is empty, the formula will not expire.
Primary application	The field is used for reporting purposes and to categorize formula types.
Product base	It is used for reporting purposes and to categorize formula items.

Table 5.10 Maintain Material Field Details

Detailed field name	Description
Position	The position number in the list of materials. The system will usually increment this value by 10. It is possible to enter a different position number than the one that is defaulted by the system.
Sequence	For each position number, the sequence number enables you to define more than one raw material. Each material listed under a different sequence number can have its own validity period.
Item	Enter the raw material item code.
Cnt (Container)	The container in which the material is packaged. This field can only be filed if the material is a containerized item.
Mat. perc. (Material percentage)	Indicates whether the material is defined as a percentage of the formula size. This field can be modified only if the field percentage formula in the session maintains formulas are set to yes. In a few instances, some raw materials can be entered in percentages while others may not (such as packing material) be so amenable. In a percentage formula, Baan enables you to enter both percentages and absolute quantities.
Net quantity	The raw material to be issued in the production of the formula item. When a production batch is planned, the actual material requirement is adjusted based on the shrinkage factor.
Un. (Unit)	The unit used for entering a quantity of a material. The system default to the product's inventory unit that was assigned in the session Maintain Item Data.
Shkg (Shrink factor)	The percentage of the material lost because of evaporation, absorption, and so on. You can prevent shortage in production by recording shrinkage.
Op (Operation)	The routing operation or step in the production process where this raw material is required. After the routing for this formula has been set up, you can enter an operation number.
Wrh (Warehouse)	The warehouse from which the raw material will be issued. This is a default warehouse that can be changed at the time of production.
Phantom	Indicates whether the raw material used is a phantom product. If so, only the raw materials that make up this product will be listed on production batch documents.
Quantity-dependent	Indicates whether the material requirements are affected by the size of the production batch. If a batch quantity is changed, the system asks whether the material quantities have to change proportionally.
Scalable	Baan can readjust the batch size if a change is made to the quantity of a scalable material.
Effective date	The first day of the validity period of the material.
Expiry date	The day on which the validity of the material expires. If the field is empty, the material will not expire.
Co-products	Enter the co-product item and quantities to be generated from the production of the main item. Note that a co-product may also have its own formula if it is further processed after it has been generated from the main item.

Maintaining co/by products: It is necessary in the process module to define the co- and by products. This is done using the session called *maintain co/by products* found in the formula management business object. A co-product will usually have a positive cost allocation because it can be sold or reused. Therefore, it can assume part of the formula cost. (Based on the benefits of this co-product, the main item costs 10 percent less or it bears only 90 percent of the cost). If costs are incurred in the disposal of a by product, however, the cost allocation can be negative. (Based on the cost of disposing of this by product, the main item costs 10 percent more to produce or it bears 110 percent of the cost.)

Maintain co/by product fields

Position: The position number of the co/by product in the list of co/by products generated in the processing of the main item.

Sequence: For each position number, the sequence number enables one to define more than one raw material. Each material listed under a different sequence number can have its own validity period (effective and expiry date).

Cnt (Container): Depending on whether the co-product is containerized, the container in which the material is packaged.

Co/By: Indicates the type of secondary item that results from the production of the main item formula.

Quantity: The co/by product output based on the formula size of the main item.

Unit: Unit in which one expresses the co/by product quantity

Cost All (cost allocation): The percentage of the total cost of the formula allocated to the co/by product. The cost allocation can be negative or positive.

Opr (Operation): The routing operation to which this co/by product is linked.

Wrh (Warehouse): The warehouse where the co/by product is stored after it has been received. This is a default warehouse that can be changed at the time of production.

Recurrent: A co/by product is recurrent if the same item is used as an ingredient in the main item formula. Ten percent of a raw material, for example, does not dissolve when it is mixed with other ingredients. The quantity is recovered at a later stage in production and received as a co-product.

Recurrent position: The value of the field position in the session Maintain Materials, where the material recovered as a co/by product is included in the main item formula.

Yield percentage: The percentage of the recurrent material anticipated to be returned from production as a recurrent co/by product.

Maintaining end-item containers: In this section, one will specify the production output in terms of packaging quantities. Here, one must determine which quantities of the main item will be packaged in each container, that is, how much of the 500 pounds of the main item will go into each container. The total units for the end items (number of containers * conversion factor) must equal the formula size displayed in the upper portion of the screen.

The end item formula is set up, based on the production of one container. The system will default the raw material quantity for the end item formula to whatever conversion exists between the inventory units of the main item and the container unit.

Maintain end item container fields

Formula item: The main item in this formula.

Formula size: The formula quantity for the main item.

Accumulated quantity: The formula quantity allotted to the containers entered in the lower portion of the screen.

Cnt (Container) : The container code in which (a part of) the formula is packaged.

Containers: Enter the quantity of each container that will be used for this formula.

Conversion factor: The conversion factor between the main item inventory unit and the container unit as set in the session maintain conversion factors.

Inventory unit: The end item quantity expressed in main item inventory unit (container quantity*conversion factor).

Seq (Sequence): Identifies the sequence in which the end items are to be packaged.

End item formulae: For containerized process items, a formula must be created for the end items.

Unique Requirements of a Process Industry

We will now discuss the typicality in the process industry and how various ERP brands address those requirements.

Formulation: The competitive advantage for companies in the process industry stems from the uniqueness of the products manufactured. This is a direct result of the formulations developed (and possibly patented) by the company. Several important requirements arise in this context; in order to maintain and enhance its standing in the company in the industry. These include:

(i) Formula security: Information on formulations needs to be under strict control, with access to formulae being a security privilege. The ability to grant rights to people at the level of each formula is extremely important.

(ii) Formula management: The composition of the formulae may need to change from time to time, due to market demands, cost considerations, etc. The ability to

revise the formula without losing history information, and switch production from one revision to the next (based on several considerations) is critical.

(iii) New product development: New products are developed, either to enhance existing formulations or to research and develop new products that will sell in the market. The ability to track the time, costs, trials and revisions, test results and comments on such projects is critical to building a powerful knowledge base of formula development history.

(iv) Lot tracking: Ability to trace from receipt of raw materials through manufacturing and to shipments of finished products is a critical requirement. Complete transparency and analysis of Lots, bi-directional Lot Tracking, and the ability to record, store and retrieve the Certificate of Analysis (CoA) of raw materials, intermediates and finished products is a fundamental requirement. These need to be addressed by management solution in a simple manner.

(v) Shelf life management: Given the perishable nature of the products, tracking shelf life of products and allocating stocks based on expiration date is necessary for efficient operations.

(vi) Product costing: Accurate assessment of the cost of finished products, considering materials, labour, activities and overheads is essential to determine the correct profitability levels of various products. The cost of products needs to be re-established on a periodic basis to keep it consistent with current market conditions.

Ramco ERP Solutions for Process Industries

Issues addressed in formulation: Ramco ERP offers powerful functionality to manage the entire lifecycle of formulations. Data level security is provided to control access to Formulations—Access can be granted or denied at the level of each and every formula. The system supports multiple revisions for the same formula, with automatic switchover of production to the new revision based on business rules. All aspects of New Product Development are tracked by the system. Projects are given a unique identification, employees associated to projects, costs are tracked against the project, and complete history including revisions, comments, tests, results, etc. are recorded. Ramco ERP features **Formulator**—a versatile formula development, costing, and laboratory analysis tool. Using this tool, new formulations can be rapidly developed by modifying and mixing existing formulae in various proportions. Using the Formulator, one can dynamically scale batch quantities, perform cost calculations, and arrive at the desired result in a quick and effective fashion.

Issues addressed in lot tracking: Ramco ERP provides the functionality for proactive, forward and backward trace ability. The information that can be readily accessed includes:

- Customers to whom a given finished product lot has been shipped
- Raw materials and the vendor lot numbers that we used to manufacture a finished product lot

- Finished product lots that have used a given raw material lot
- Access to Certificate of Analysis (CoA) for raw materials and finished products alike machines, labour and accessories used in the manufacture of a finished product lot.

Issues addressed in shelf life: Ramco ERP is designed to track shelf life on all lot controlled items and automatically suggest a retest. The system automatically 'holds' the stock that has gone past the expiration date so that such lots are not inadvertently consumed or shipped. The application also supports multiple allocation methods for material issue transactions, including 'Expiration date based' and 'FIFO'.

Issues addressed in product costing: Ramco ERP supports ABC costing techniques to accurately roll-up the cost of the product from the cost of raw material, labour and activities. The entire process of cost simulations, cost roll-up and inventory revaluation at the then prevailing standard cost is supported by the system.

The formula management module/software facilitates *automatic formulation information* transfer between *shop floor and R&D* department. This enables leveraging of past and current R&D knowledge, faster and less expensive *new product development*, and easier attainment of product quality standards. It is especially useful as the main requirement of the food companies is constantly bringing new products into the market. The module provides necessary security for the formula by allowing only authorized access. This way, the efficient handling of co/by products is ensured and the unique characteristics of the process industry are accounted for.

FINANCIAL ACCOUNTING MODULE IN ERP

Financial accounting indicates the overall performance of the management of the enterprise. Normally, it is the preparation and communication of financial information to be used predominantly by people outside the organization. This is done by preparing three major financial statements for a particular period.

1. **The profit and loss account** for a specific accounting period reports the results of operations of an enterprise during that period.
2. **The balance sheet** which shows the financial position of the enterprise at the end of the same period.
3. **The statement of cash flows** which summarizes cash inflows and outflows of the business enterprise during a specific accounting period.

The file or binder that contains the entire group of accounts of a business is called a **ledger**. The major sections in the ledger are assets, liabilities, shareholder's equity, revenues and expenses. A complete listing of account numbers and the associated account titles is called **chart of accounts**.

To handle all the requirements mentioned above, ERP uses Financial Accounting Module which consists of the following major components:

1. General ledger
2. Accounts receivable
3. Accounts payable
4. Asset accounting

We will now analyze how these issues are addressed in various ERP products.

Financial Accounting in Oracle ERP

The financial applications of the Oracle ERP suite of applications are the General Ledger and the subledgers. In addition, the Inventory (INV), Cost Management (CST), and Purchasing (PO) applications can also make journal entries in the General Ledger, but these applications are more properly classified as manufacturing or distribution applications.

Oracle takes into account the accounting equation principle and the transaction principle. The accounting equation states that the total assets must equal total liabilities and owner's equity. The transaction principle states that all financial transactions must be recorded and balanced. A full audit trail from the Oracle General Ledger is available. Figure 5.3 shows the GL module relationships with other applications.

Oracle GL journal entry balance types include actual journals and budget journals. Actual journals post to either a financial currency or statistical currency. Journal sources define the subsystem, and journal categories define the module within the subsystem, e.g. journal source is payables and journal category is payments. In addition, a journal approval process may be defined and journals may automatically post a periodic request to select and post certain journal sources and categories.

Oracle general ledger journal capabilities also include recurring journals and allocation journals. Recurring data journals speed data entry by automatically creating the journal. They allow cost pools to be distributed across the organization. They may be run in parallel mode, or in step down mode, which means allocations are run in a cascading fashion. For example, the first level journal is generated before the next level allocation journal.

Oracle GL budget capabilities include online budget entry, a number of mathematical formulas, and the ability to load budgets from any other system. In addition, mass budgeting allows the organization to create budgets or forecasts based on actual data.

Oracle GL provides online inquiry and reporting capabilities. The drill-down from account inquiry to the Oracle application subsystem to the T-accounts and journal entry transactions is phenomenal. This drill-down functionality is available for Oracle application subsystems including payables, receivables, assets, projects, inventory and WIP.

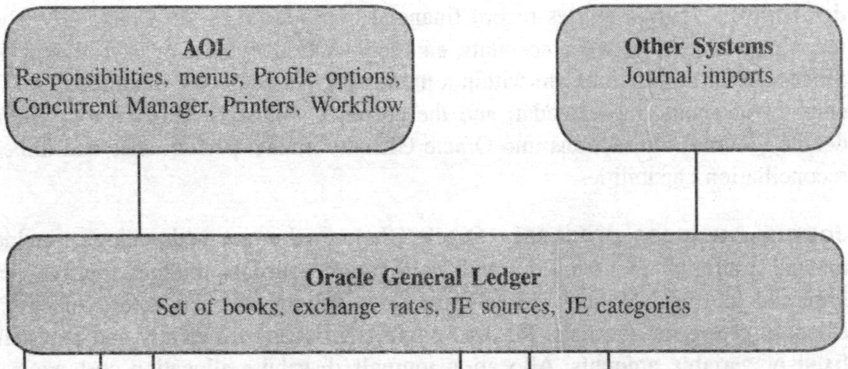

Figure 5.3 Oracle GL: General ledger relationships to other applications.

Oracle GL provides standard General Ledger reports as with any other Oracle application. In addition, it provides a user reporting tool called *Financial Statement Generator (FSG)* which allows the user to develop custom financial reports from the posted account balances.

Journals include manually entered journals as well as those imported from Oracle applications or legacy systems. These amounts are considered actual balance types.

Budget capabilities include manual budget entry as well as those budgets imported from a budget legacy system. These budget amounts are considered budget balance types. Both balance types must update the GL balance records before inquiry, and reporting will display the proper amounts.

The Oracle GL account inquiry window drill downs from GL balances to journals, which created the balance to the Oracle applications that created the journal entry. In addition, the journal accounts are graphically represented.

We will now discuss various submodules available in Oracle and SAP GL module.

Journals: Journal entries record financial transactions to the Oracle GL. They record movements between accounts, e.g. depreciation expense or payroll expense. Since journal transactions are within a unique GL set of books, the three C's—the chart of accounts, the calendar, and the currency—must be adhered to. Sending detailed journal transactions into Oracle GL may impact performance and impede reconciliation capabilities.

Journal business process: Oracle GL journal entry methodologies include manual journals, recurring journals, allocation journals, budget journals and imported journals. Manual journals are those entered when no other subsystem exists to create the journals. Recurring journals occur periodically and may have fixed or variable amounts. Allocation journals distribute allocation cost pools to various accounts based on usage ratios. Budget journals insert or update budget data. Imported journals are journals created in a subsystem outside Oracle GL (e.g. conversion journals); they also include Oracle Payables and Oracle receivables journals.

Oracle payables: Oracle Payables journal provides the standard supplier, invoice and payment processes. Also, it provides payables capabilities with procurement card and EDI functionality. Further, Oracle's web applications allow users outside Oracle applications to enter their data, for example, self service applications.

Payables business process flow: First, an Oracle Payables environment must be defined. Suppliers must be defined before an invoice may be entered. Likewise, an invoice must be entered and approved before a payment may be created or entered. Both transactions create journal entries to Oracle General Ledger.

Oracle receivables: Oracle Receivable System is used to track customers, customer transactions, receipts, and collection activities. Oracle Receivables also prints invoices, credit memos, dunning letters, and statements. Full collection capabilities with a complete audit trail are also available.

Oracle Receivables is an open receivables system, not a balance forward receivable system. An open item receivable system links all receivable activities to the original transaction. The original transaction has an open status until the sum of transaction activities equals zero, such as a full credit memo. A transaction will be reversed if an activity causes the balance to not equal zero, such as a reversed receipt.

Oracle receivables business process flow: The Oracle Receivables environment must be defined for the operating unit organization.

Customers must be defined before an invoice and/or receipt may be entered. If a receipt is to be applied to an invoice, the invoice must be entered first. Inquiry and reporting allow the collection personnel to record customer calls and other contact information. At period-end, the financial transactions should be transferred to create Oracle GL journal entries.

SAP R/3 Financial Accounting

The major parts of financial accounting in SAP R/3 are:

1. General Ledger
2. Accounts Receivable
3. Accounts Payable
4. Asset Accounting
5. Closing and Reporting
6. Financial Information System

General ledger: The central task of GL accounting is to provide a comprehensive picture of external accounting and accounts. Recording all business transactions in a software system which is fully integrated with all the other operational areas of a company ensures that the accounting data is always complete and accurate. The general ledger serves as a complete record of all business transactions. It is the centralized, up-to-date reference for the rendering of accounts. Actual individual transactions can be checked at any time in real time processing by displaying the original documents, line items and monthly debits and credits at various levels such as accounts, journals, summary balance sheet, and profit and loss account. For every GL account, we need to create a master record. A master record contains information that tells how to enter and post business transactions to the appropriate account and then process the data that is posted. Figure 5.4 gives a pictorial view of the SAP GL module relationship with other modules.

Some of the features of the GL module are:

- Automatic and simultaneous posting of all subledger items in the appropriate general ledger accounts
- Simultaneous updating of general ledger and cost accounting areas
- Inter-company transactions

The system assures the integration of subledgers with FI general ledger accounting, e.g. when a customer account is posted, the system automatically makes a posting to the corresponding reconciliation account in the general ledger. Standard reconciliation accounts are:

- Domestic payables or receivables
- Payables to or receivables from affiliated companies
- Foreign payables or receivables

Whenever transactions are posted to the accounts in the form of documents, it is necessary that they be "complete" (Balance of debit and credit items are zero) along with the account number, amount, etc. Some entries such as tax and gain/loss from foreign exchange rates are entered by the system automatically.

We will now discuss a few submodules of the SAP Finance module.

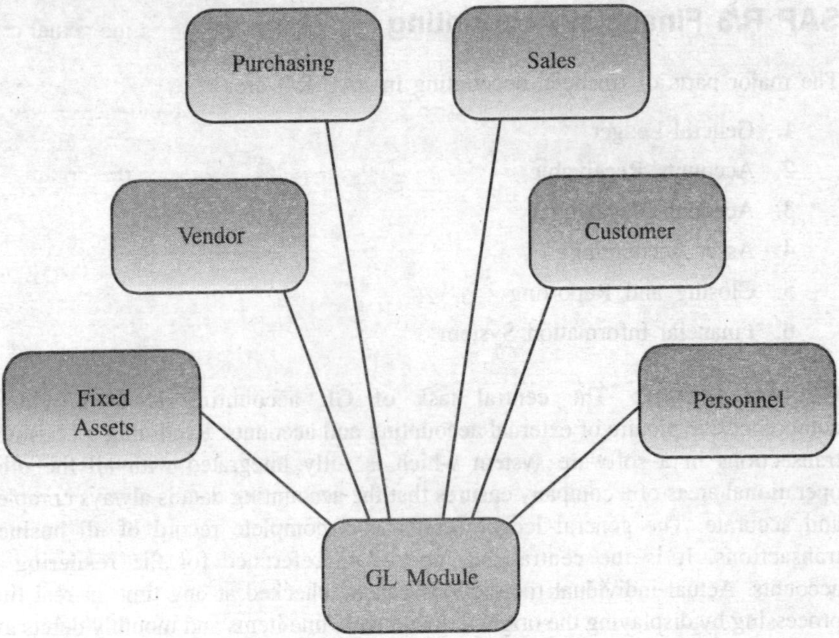

Figure 5.4 SAP GL module.

Accounts receivable: The accounts receivable subledger maintains an account of the value owed to the company and shares the chart of accounts and the details of master records. It is fully integrated with the sales and distribution module giving effective credit management and is also closely linked to the Cash Management module. There are a number of tools available such as balance lists, journals, balance audit trails, and allocation of payments via screens or EDI. Some of the special transactions are:

(i) Down payments: These are shown separately from receivables since payment is posted even when goods have not been delivered. It represents an obligation to deliver.

(ii) Bill of exchange: The customers pay via bill of exchange and get a longer payment period (3 months).

(iii) Guarantees made: Credit management: Based on the customer type, the user can set a credit limit for the customer. So the limit is checked each time an amount is posted to the customer account.

Credit limits can be set at different levels, always related to a single customer.

(i) Total credit limit: This determines the total permissible credit for a customer across all credit control areas.

(ii) Maximum individual credit limit. This limit sets a ceiling on the amount of credit that may be granted to the customer in any one credit control area in the system.

(iii) Individual credit limit. The individual credit limit determines the actual credit limit for a certain customer in a certain control area.

The SAP/R3 system also keeps a note of all correspondences with the customers including payment notices, balance confirmations, etc. It also has a facility called "dunning" which reminds customers that they owe the organization money for overdue invoices. Dunning is carried out automatically using the dunning program. The program determines the accounts and items to be dunned, the dunning level of the account, and the dunning notice based on the dunning level.

Accounts payable: The Accounts Payable application component records accounting data for all vendors. It is also an integral part of Purchasing. The system automatically makes postings to the FI component in response to purchase transactions. The system is linked to the Cash Management application component and provides figures from invoices for liquidity planning. Outstanding payables are settled by the payment program. This program supports all standard payment methods in printed form as well as in electronic form. This program also covers payment methods specific to different countries.

Postings made in Accounts Payable are simultaneously recorded in the General Ledger, where different G/L accounts are updated based on the transaction involved (payables, down payments, and so on). The vendor master record controls how transactions are posted for a given vendor. The same master record is used for the Materials Management module as well. Similar to the accounts receivable there are special transactions:

1. Bill of Exchange payable
2. Guarantees
3. Down payments

The module also has a check management facility that provides for use of prenumbered cheques, which are allowed in countries like USA and Australia. It also provides the following correspondence methods—payment notices with or without line items, account statements and open item lists.

Asset accounting: The Asset Accounting module consists of the following components:

1. Traditional asset accounting
2. Leasing
3. Preparation for consolidation
4. Information system

Asset accounting provides for the value of the assets over their entire lifetime. It has capabilities to capture depreciation, interest and insurance. It provides a report for depreciation forecasting. It permits different kinds of valuation and offers special functions for leased assets and assets under construction. In addition, the valuation can be country specific. The depreciation charts can be country specific. For internal accounting purposes, asset costs have to be assigned to cost centres. This way the depreciation charge for the given period can be allocated to the cost centre at the end of the depreciation period. Fixed assets can be structured into levels according to classes (based on legal requirements) or asset grouping for common evaluation. Assets under construction are considered to be special kinds of tangible assets and are shown as separate items in the balance sheet. Similarly, the system provides for low value assets that fully depreciate in the period of purchase, leased assets, intangible assets, financial assets (managed by the treasury component) and technical assets. Depreciation methods available are Percentage rate from useful life, Total percentage rate in the tax concession period, Explicit percentage rate, Percentage rate from remaining life + Changeover date – depreciation start date, Mean value from several areas, Unit-of-production method of depreciation, Depreciation over remaining units of production, Sum-of-the-years-digits method, Depreciation according to the present value of lease installments, Declining-balance method of depreciation according to Japanese regulations.

Closing and reporting: *The closing operations include* periodic accrual and deferral of expenditures and revenues, recording and valuating payables and receivables, creating the balance sheet and the profit and loss statement, and documenting the posting data.

The closing operations can be subdivided into:

- Day-end closing
- Month-end closing
- Year-end closing

Financial information system: The financial information system enables you to evaluate the general ledger, accounts receivable, and accounts payable. Its primary database is the Financial Accounting application. The Financial Information System job is to provide data from the above database and give it to user's in an easy-to-read form. It is possible to analyze payment history, currency exposure among customers and vendors, or aging reports. The GL account transaction figures as well as the balance sheet, and the P&L structures serve as the primary database for the general ledger information system. Analysis can be done on a quarterly, half yearly or full yearly basis.

Some of the key figures that can be tracked are profits (such as annual net profit) and payment resources like "cash flow", equity ratio, debt-equity ratio, and capitalization intensity.

MASTER PRODUCTION SCHEDULING (MPS) MODULE IN ERP

Master Production Scheduling is defined as an anticipated build schedule for manufacturing end items or product options by quantity per planning period (called the time buckets). It represents what the company plans to produce, expressed in specific configurations, quantities and dates. As already discussed, S&OP process authorizes MPS module various products that should be translated into the MPS. Thus, MPS is a listing of the end items (products) or major subassemblies (standard modules) which are to be produced in known quantity and when they should be ready for shipment or further value addition.

MPS is a logical representation of information for decision-making. It is what the firm or plant expects to produce in the short run. Each individual MPS has a supporting BoM or Formula defining the components needed to produce the planned quantities of the end item. Thus, MPS becomes the inputs to MRP.

Typically, MPS in ERP provides the intelligence to interpret the signals it gets from sales and forecast, to think of alternative means of satisfying customer demands, and to make adjustments in capacity, inventories and so forth, and allow the company to serve the customer without imbalance between supply and demand.

Objectives of MPS Module

- Develop data (MPS) to drive detailed planning (MRP II).
- Provide devices to reconcile customer's desires with plant, material and vendor capabilities.
- Furnish means to make reliable delivery promises and to evaluate the effects of schedule changes.
- Coordinate plans and actions of all organization functions and measure their performance.
- Provide management with means to authorize and control all resources needed to support integrated plans.
- Schedule production orders and purchase orders for MPS items.

Functions of MPS Module

MPS have two principal functions:

(i) In the short horizon: To serve as bases for planning material requirements, production of components, order priorities, and short-term capacity requirements. The function relates to the 'firm' (front end) period of the MPS, which is usually equal to the sum of production lead-times from release of purchase requisition to completion of MPS level items. The following are the functions performed:

(a) *RCCP check:* The MPS process limits the work to what can be realistically done

(b) *Production smoothing:* It buffers the forecast by 'smoothing' demand over time, reducing capacity-constrained peaks, and raising low-demand idle periods.

(c) *Netting:* It subcontracts existing inventories of products from the forecast so that the shop does not make products that already exist in the inventory.

(d) *Lot sizing:* MPS divides demands over time into convenient and economical groups for production so that scarce facilities and equipment are not wasted.

(ii) Over the long horizon: To serve as bases for estimating long-term demands on company resources such as people, plant and equipment, warehousing and capital.

MPS Control for Items

Items in MPS are generally the end items, defined as highest-level entities—components of any parent. However, shippable products, major assemblies, planning modules, and group of components covered by fake bills may also be included in the MPS.

The nature of the manufacturing environment (MTS/ATO/MTO) is a critical determinant of the MPS process. We see the various patterns of product structures, namely, funnel (V plant), pyramid (A plant), and hourglass (T plant) associated with various manufacturing environments. ERP recommends the MPS-point in the product structure that gives the *maximum control with the fewest items to master-schedule*, as master scheduling is the highly leveraged activity.

Master Scheduling Activities

All the activities in MPS must result in an aggregate plan aimed at keeping aggregate balance between supply and demand and accordingly making the shipments. Three main activities involved in MPS module of ERP are:

- Designing of MPS
- Generation of MPS
- Control of MPS

These are now briefly described.

Designing the MPS: It includes the following steps:

1. Select the items to be master scheduled. This involves selecting the levels in the BoM structure to be represented by the items scheduled (both components and final assemblies may be included)
2. Organize the MPS by product groups.
3. Determine the planning horizon, the time fences, and the related operational guides.
4. Select the method for calculating and presenting the available-to-promise (ATP) information.

Creating MPS: It includes the following steps:

1. Obtain the necessary informational inputs. This includes the forecast, the backlog (customer commitments), and the inventory on hand.
2. Prepare the initial draft of the MPS.
3. Develop the rough-cut capacity plan (RCCP).
4. If required, increase capacity or revise the initial draft. This process is repeated until the time feasible MPS is obtained.

Controlling the MPS: It includes the following activities:

1. Track actual production and compare it to planned production to determine if the planned MPS quantities and promises to deliver are being met.
2. Calculate the ATP to determine if an assurance can be given to meet an incoming order within a specific period.
3. Calculate the project on hand to determine if planned production is sufficient to fill expected future orders.
4. Use the results of the preceding activities to determine if the MPS or capacity should be revised.

Figure 5.5 shows the actual screen shot of Forecasting Module of an ERP Product. Thus the MPS module triggers the MRP and CRP modules for further processing.

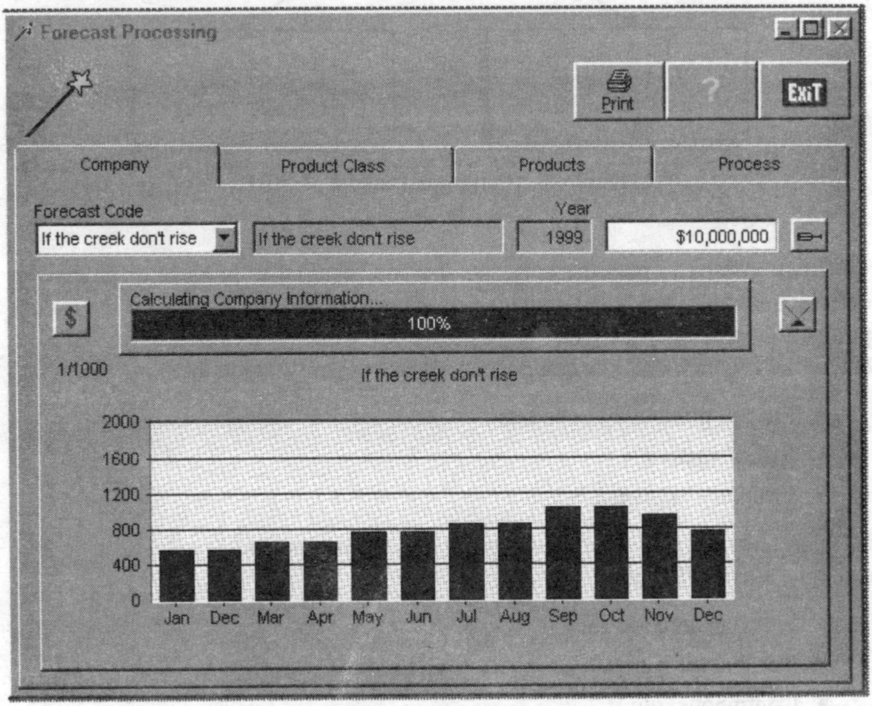

Figure 5.5 Screen shot of forecasting module of an ERP product.

MATERIAL REQUIREMENT PLANNING (MRP) MODULE IN ERP

This technique originated way back in 1962–65 but is still at the heart of the ERP concept, and hence its is observed in every ERP product. It is basically used to balance supply with demand, automating the creation of new supply/work orders, and regulating the inventory levels. Figures 5.6 and 5.7 show the basic approach followed in MRP.

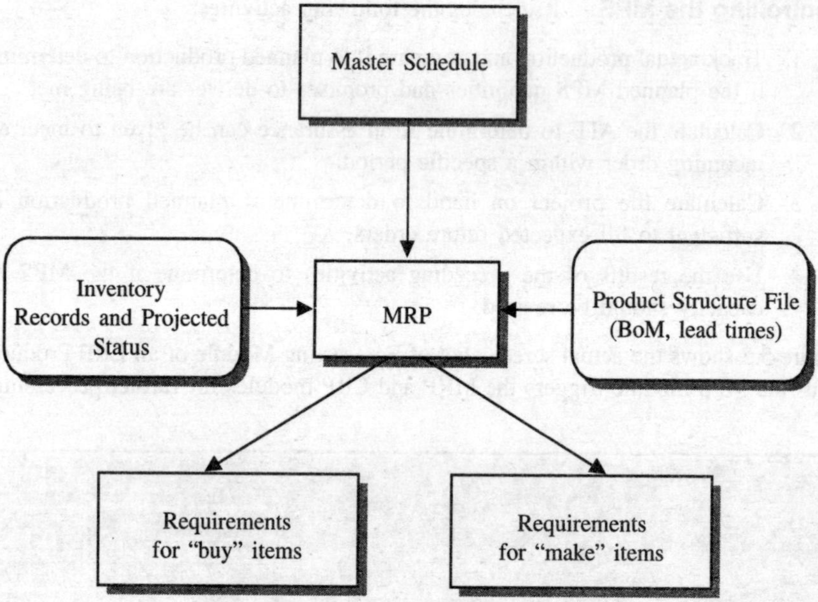

Figure 5.6 Conceptual model of MRP.

MRP is used to plan the materials that are required to produce or procure in definite quantities and at determined time, based on the specification in the master production schedule. In fact, its basic model works backwards from MPS to determine requirements for components. It uses mainly inputs like:

- Master production schedule
- Bill of materials
- Inventory database

MRP is featured with its running modes and order policies available in it. For example, Baan MRP has:

- Full regeneration run
- Net change run
- Continuous run

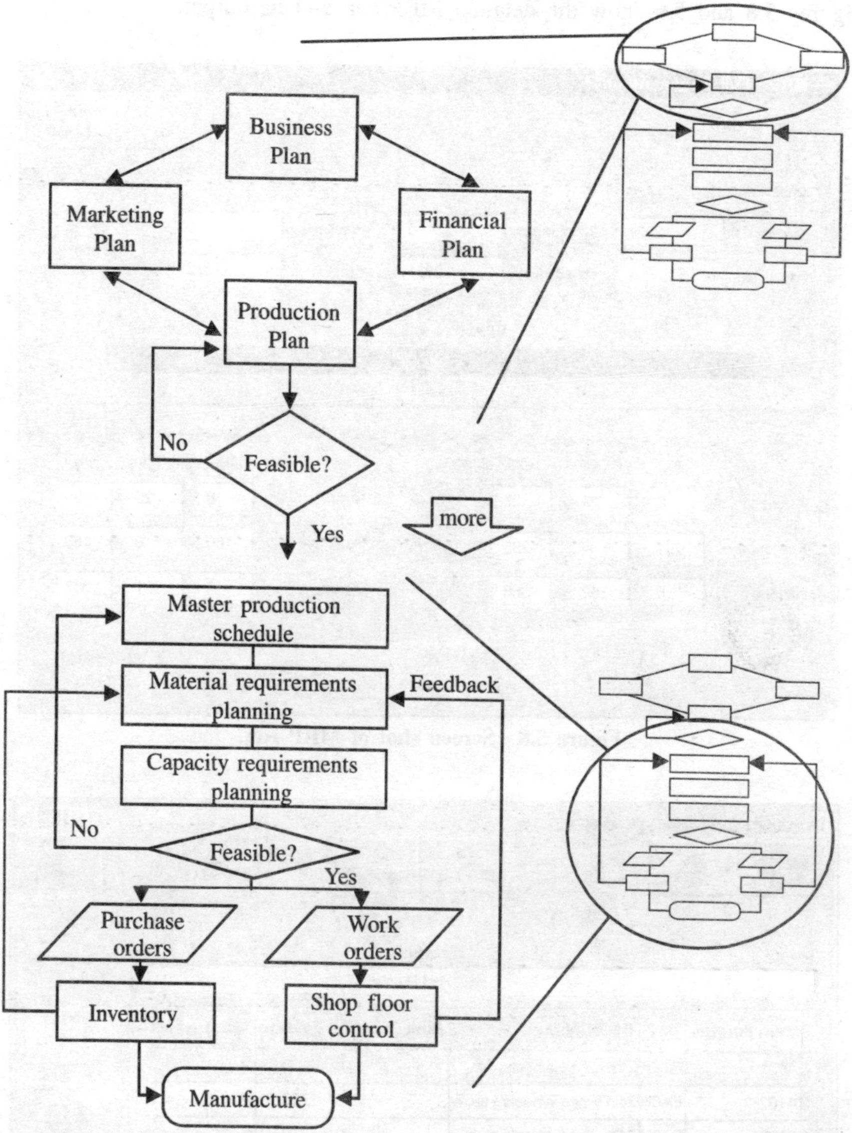

Figure 5.7 Conceptual model of relationships between MPS, MRP & CRP.

The order policies supported are:

- Fixed order quantity
- Lot for lot
- Fixed period of supply
- Reorder point.

Figures 5.8 and 5.9 show the detailed MRP run and its output.

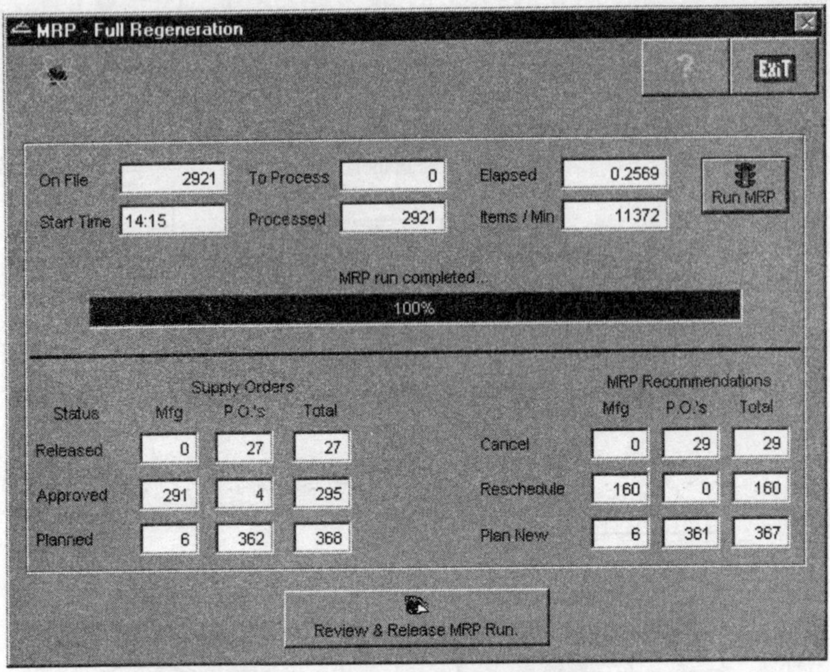

Figure 5.8 Screen shot of MRP run.

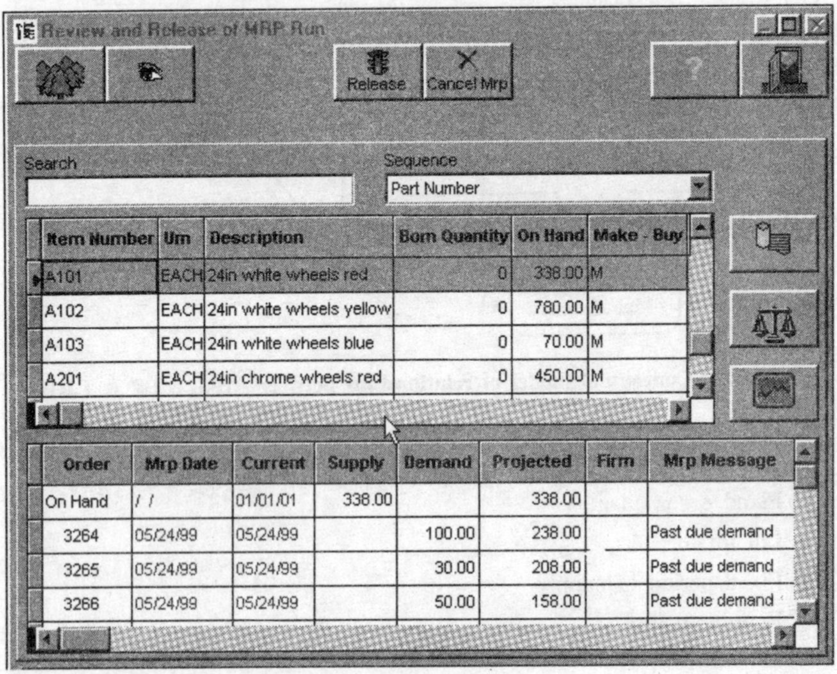

Figure 5.9 Output of MRP run.

MRP maintains the time-phased control on every purchase, inventory and production activity. It manages inventory levels by planning according to demand generated by a combination of customer orders and sales forecasts. Forecasts are managed in the MPS module or, optionally, developed offline and imported into the system. This is necessary for the *long lead items* handled by *MRP Forecast Module*.

Production Scheduling

MRP schedules the orders by capacity and order priority. It supports infinite scheduling options with shop calendar constraint that can go to the machine level. It can also facilitate selectable backlog prioritization and changes in routines. Bottleneck work centers can be reported and graphical analysis is supported in most of the ERP products. Figure 5.10 shows the manufacturing schedule generated in ERP.

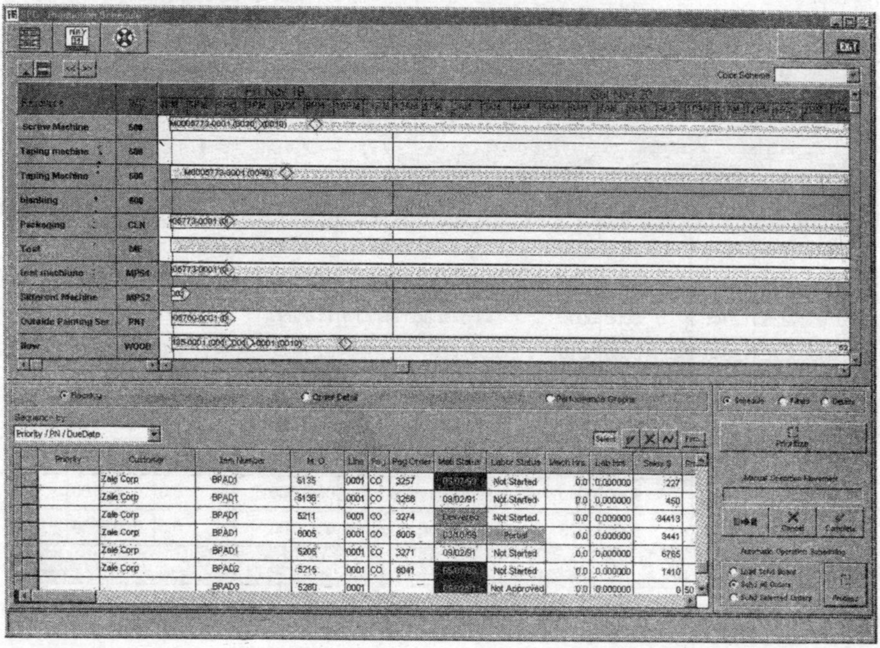

Figure 5.10 Screen shot of manufacturing schedule generated in ERP.

MRP also gets information from real time **Shop Floor Control Module** that manages the production environment by carrying out the following activities:

1. Using MRP outputs and schedules for production, people and equipment
2. Identifying material shortages
3. Recording direct and indirect labour
4. Offering interactive operator job reporting

5. Collecting information for historical performance reporting by item, operator, and operation
6. Supporting creation of an electronic batch record of each production order
7. Allowing detailed reporting or back flushing for material and labour reporting.

ERP never encourages manual entry of manufacturing orders (Work Orders), but MRP and sales order processing should automatically set them up, saving a lot of time and effort. Figure 5.11 shows the production order completion note generated in ERP.

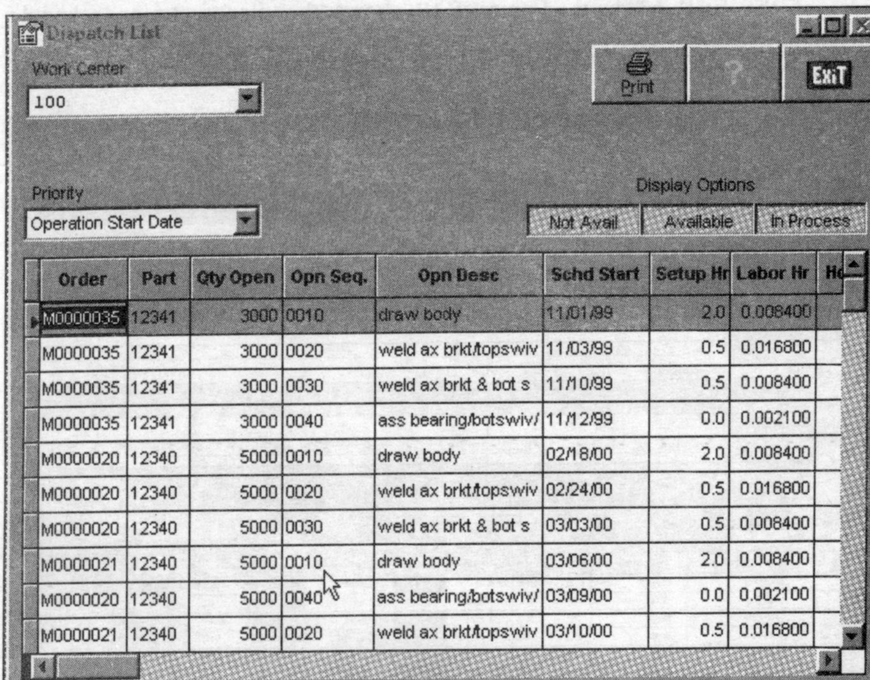

Order	Part	Qty Open	Opn Seq.	Opn Desc	Schd Start	Setup Hr	Labor Hr
M0000035	12341	3000	0010	draw body	11/01/99	2.0	0.008400
M0000035	12341	3000	0020	weld ax brkt/topswiv	11/03/99	0.5	0.016800
M0000035	12341	3000	0030	weld ax brkt & bot s	11/10/99	0.5	0.008400
M0000035	12341	3000	0040	ass bearing/botswiv/	11/12/99	0.0	0.002100
M0000020	12340	5000	0010	draw body	02/18/00	2.0	0.008400
M0000020	12340	5000	0020	weld ax brkt/topswiv	02/24/00	0.5	0.016800
M0000020	12340	5000	0030	weld ax brkt & bot s	03/03/00	0.5	0.008400
M0000021	12340	5000	0010	draw body	03/06/00	2.0	0.008400
M0000020	12340	5000	0040	ass bearing/botswiv/	03/09/00	0.0	0.002100
M0000021	12340	5000	0020	weld ax brkt/topswiv	03/10/00	0.5	0.016800

Figure 5.11 Screen shot of production order completion note.

The standard process is:

1. Orders are planned to cover customer and production requirements.
2. Production material shortages are covered by orders to vendors.
3. Messages are created identifying item, priority, and release timing.
4. Orders are reviewed and released by the planner.
5. Released orders are moved to the production mix.
6. Schedule revisions are communicated to production in real time.

CRP MODULE IN ERP

Capacity Requirements Planning is a tool which is used to determine the available and required capacity to help alleviate bottlenecks as well as identify potential problems before they occur. This technique in ERP concept is basically used to predict resource requirements for critical workstations, called *RCCP* (Rough Cut Capacity Planning). Several components are input into the system to effectively address the capacity and planning needs for instance:

- Planned order releases
- Routing file
- Open orders file.

The outputs of CRP are the load profile for each work center.

ERP assumes certain terms related to CRP. For example:

- **Planned order releases:** Information from MRP which tells you when you should start the order so that can be completed on time. The planned order release is from the material requirements planning which translates a master schedule for end items into time-phased requirements for subassemblies, components and raw materials. It is used to ensure that certain materials are available when needed.
- **Routing files:** Information that details the requirements of equipment and labour to complete the order as needed in the required timeframe. Routing file has a triple component—it determines which workers and/or machines are needed for an order, which operations should be completed first, and the length of time each operation will take.
- **Open orders files:** Information regarding the orders that are currently started and need to be completed. Open order files contain the data on the jobs currently being worked on but are not yet completed.
- **Capacity** is the maximum output or volume a system can produce—the maximum work that a system is capable of doing in a given period of time. This information is needed to determine the projects that companies can commit themselves to, bid on or accept. By calculating the capacity, the company can determine whether they are capable of completing the project within the timeframe required.

Let us now discuss the CRP module of Navision, the popular ERP product by Microsoft. Figure 5.12 shows the scope of CRP module in Navision ERP.

The primary objectives of CRP module are:

- Maximize facility utilization
- Create realistic production plan
- Monitor current work-in-progress
- Display scheduled load
- Perform 'what-if' analysis

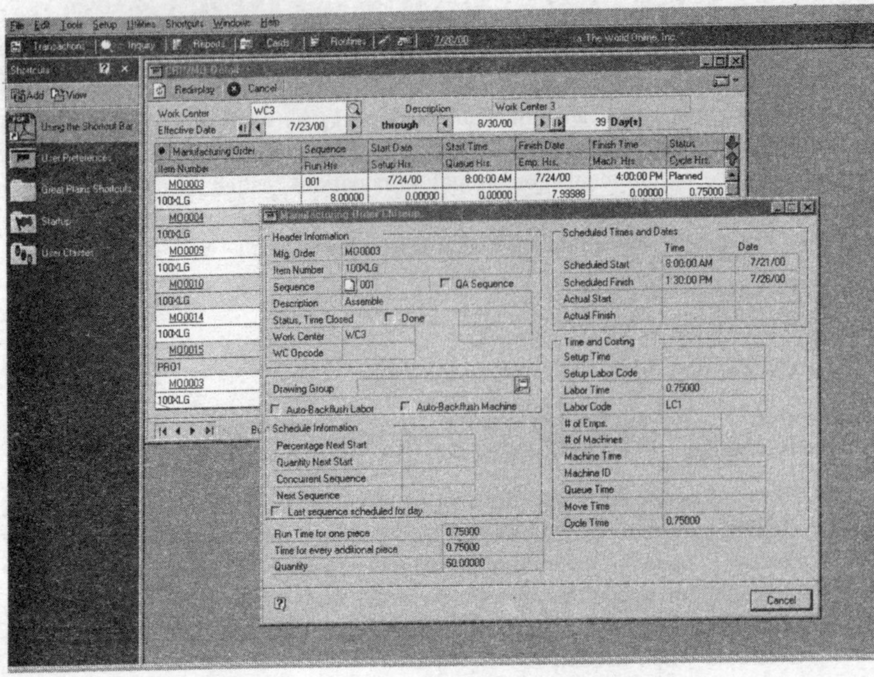

Figure 5.12 Screen shot of CRP module in Microsoft Navision.

- Selectively use forward or backward scheduling
- Calculate capacity to match run time requirements.

Navision provides the following functionalities in CRP:

(i) Basic capacity planning

- Shop calendar and work shifts
- Routings
- Parallel scheduling
- "Send ahead" functionality for Just-in-Time (JIT) production
- Routing link codes for automatic flushing per operational steps on the routing
- Scrap and stop codes can be defined to reduce data entry
- Automatic flushing of the work or machine center provides automatic recording of expected output
- Subcontracting by work center or operation

(ii) Management machine centers: Allocates work and machine centers as capacities to the manufacturing process.

(iii) Finite loading: Finite loading of capacity constrained resources (Capacity constraints taken into account to help planners make more reliable plans).

The two modules, visual resource planner and work center load report, carry out the above-mentioned procedures.

Visual Resource Planner

The CRP module uses a visual interface that allows you to view and change the schedule for any shop order. It provides the capability to graphically display the load in each work center, highlighting the shop orders that have insufficient machine or labour hour capacity. Shop order detail, work center capacity and work center load graphs are easily accessible through menu options or push buttons.

Using the intuitive visual interface, shop orders scheduled for an operation on a given day can be moved to a different day or operation by dragging and dropping the shop order. The visual interface provides sufficient warnings when due dates are being impacted or operations are moved out of sequence. Any schedule changes are saved to "What-If" files for later analysis. Once the desired schedule changes are made, a process update feature will update the database with the transactions from the selected 'What-If' file. Figure 5.13 depicts the what-if analysis module.

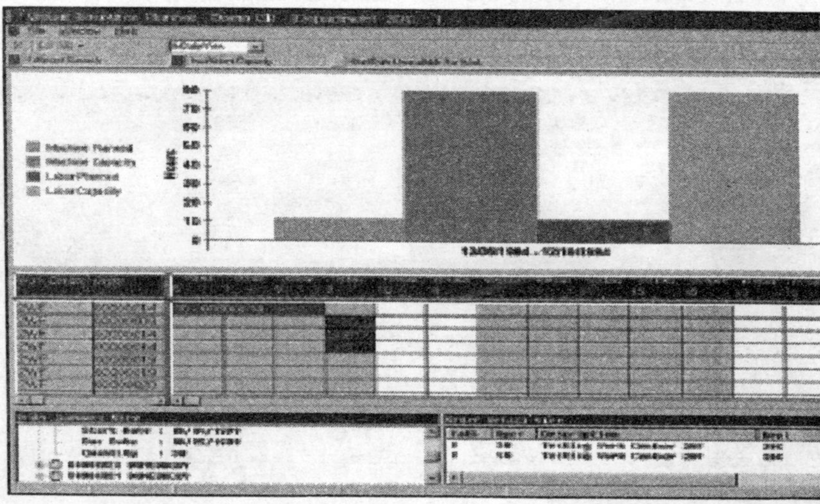

Figure 5.13 Illustration of what-if analysis.

CRP stores orders in a Simulated Load file so that the user may alter them without affecting the original orders. Along these same lines, CRP also provides the ability to add, modify and delete firm planned orders and to convert computer planned orders into firm planned orders. It also provides visual tools that enable the planner to adjust the schedule so that it accommodates capacity in a better way.

Once orders have been merged into the Simulated Load file, they can be modified to accomplish rescheduling. The user may change the scheduling method for an order as well as its start and due dates to investigate alternative solutions to the problem of inadequate capacity.

Changes to the start date of a non-dependent shop order can have repercussions if the order requires components that are produced by other shop orders. CRP is able to reschedule dependent shop orders based on changes made to the start date of the highest-level (non-dependent) order. Such rescheduling helps ensure that components will be ready when they are needed.

Once a schedule with an acceptable load profile has been established, the scheduling information can be posted back to the packages from which the orders were copied using the Post Schedule Updates application. However, posting is optional. CRP can be used successfully to merely model the data in an effort to improve the master schedule, but complex changes to the schedule really require the automatic updating that the posting application provides.

Capacity Requirements Planning shows graphically the load that exists in a particular work center during a particular period of time based on the existing schedule. The planner can quickly determine if capacity is adequate to accommodate the projected load. It is this report and the ability to modify scheduling information in isolation from the active orders that constitute CRP's "What If Modelling" capabilities. The planner can modify the schedule and run the Work Center Load Graph over and over in an effort to even out the load on the work center. Figure 5.14 shows the work center loading.

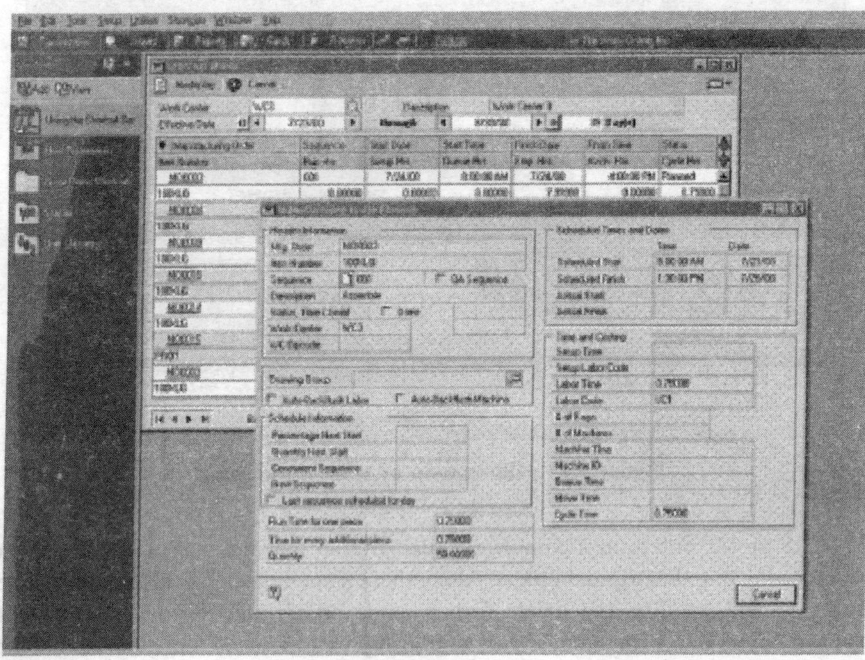

Figure 5.14 Work center load graph.

Work Center Load Report

The Work Center Load Report presents the same data as the Work Center Load Graph except that it shows detailed information about those orders that contribute to the load. For quicker access, the Work Center Load Inquiry application displays a summarized version of the same data.

PURCHASE CONTROL MODULE IN ERP

As explained already, purchasing starts only when *purchase requisitions* are generated in ERP systems ideally through MRP run. The ERP concept never encourages the buying of anything without valid requisition. The standard purchasing flow in ERP is as follows:

- Orders are planned to cover customer and production requirements.
- Messages are created identifying item, priority, and release timing.
- Orders are reviewed; vendors, quantities, terms are changed and approved.
- Orders are sent to the vendor via fax, e-mail, EDI, or hardcopy.
- Receiving processes inbound material according to quality specifications.
- Receiving routes material based on production and customer requirements.
- Accounts payable is updated from the receiving process.

We will now discuss various steps in the Materials Management Module of SAP. The typical procurement cycle for a service or material consists of seven phases which we now describe.

1. Determination of requirements: Materials requirements are identified either in the user departments or via materials planning and control. (This can cover both MRP proper and the demand-based approach to inventory control. The regular checking of stock levels of materials defined by master records, use of the order-point method, and forecasting on the basis of past usage are important aspects of the latter.) One can enter purchase requisitions, or these can be generated automatically by the materials planning and control system.

2. Source determination: The purchasing component helps one to identify potential sources of supply based on past orders and existing longer-term purchase agreements. This speeds up the process of creating requests for quotation (RFQs), which can be sent to vendors electronically via SAP EDI, if desired.

3. Vendor selection and comparison of quotations: The system is capable of simulating pricing scenarios, allowing one to compare a number of different quotations. Rejection letters can be sent automatically.

4. Purchase order processing: The purchasing system adopts information from the requisition and the quotation to help one create a purchase order. As with purchase requisitions, one can generate POs himself or have the system generate them automatically. Vendor scheduling agreements and contracts (in the SAP System, types of longer-term purchase agreement) are also supported.

5. Purchase order follow-up: The system checks the reminder periods one has specified and, if necessary, automatically prints reminders or expediters at the predefined intervals. It also provides one with an up-to-date status of all purchase requisitions, quotations, and purchase orders.

6. Goods receiving and inventory management: Goods receiving personnel can confirm the receipt of goods simply by entering the PO number. By specifying permissible tolerances, buyers can limit over- and under-deliveries of ordered goods.

7. Invoice verification: The system supports the checking and matching of invoices. The accounts payable clerk is notified of quantity and price variances because the system has access to PO and goods receipt data. This speeds the process of auditing and clearing invoices for payment.

The Purchasing Document

A purchasing document is an instrument used by purchasing to procure materials or services. The following list shows the various purchasing documents available in the standard SAP system.

(i) Request for Quotation (RFQ): A request for quotation (RFQ) is an invitation extended to a vendor by a purchasing organization to submit a quotation (bid) for the supply of materials or performance of services.

(ii) Quotation: A quotation is an offer by a vendor to a purchasing organization regarding the supply of materials or performance of services subject to specified conditions.

(iii) Purchase order (PO): It is buying entity's request or instruction to a vendor (external supplier) to supply certain materials or render/perform certain services/works, formalizing a purchase transaction. Figure 5.15 shows the screen shot of PO entry in ERP.

(iv) Contract: In the SAP purchasing component, this is a type of "outline agreement", or longer-term buying arrangement. The contract is a binding commitment to procure a certain material or service from a vendor over a certain period of time.

(v) Scheduling agreement: This is another type of "outline agreement" or longer-term buying arrangement. Scheduling agreements provide for the creation of delivery schedules specifying purchase quantities, delivery dates, and possibly also precise times of delivery over a predefined period.

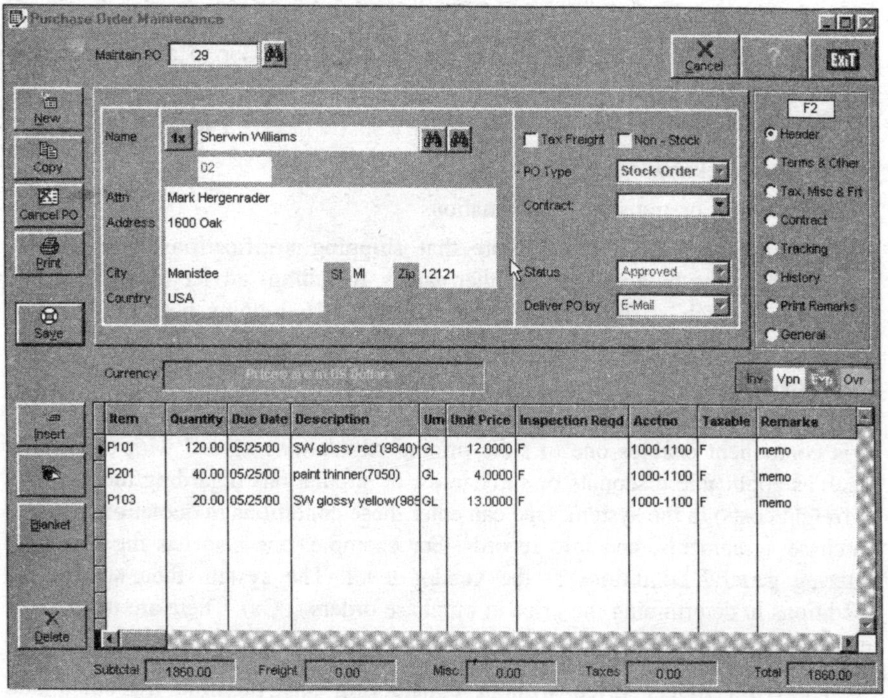

Figure 5.15 Screenshot purchase order maintenance in ERP.

Structure of Purchasing Document

Each purchasing document is subdivided into two main areas: the header and individual items. Each document will contain a header and can contain several items.

The header contains information relevant to the whole document. The items specify the materials or services to be procured. For example, information about the vendor and the document number is contained in the document header, and the material description and the order quantity are specified in each item.

Purchasing Functions

Reporting in purchasing: Those with ultimate responsibility for purchasing operations within an enterprise frequently need to obtain an overview of their vendors and purchasing organizations. The reports and analyses available in the SAP System provide this overview in a fast and straightforward manner, allowing senior executives to react appropriately to given situations. Reports can be generated on the basis of purchase order No., vendor, tracking No., material code, etc.

Vendor confirmations: In purchasing, the term *confirmation* is an umbrella term for various kinds of information provided by a vendor to a customer with regard to ordered goods.

The possible types of confirmation include the following:

- Order acknowledgments
- Loading or transport confirmations
- Shipping notifications. [Note that shipping notifications may also be referred to by a number of other names, including "advice (note)", "advice of dispatch", "ship notice", and "advance (d) shipping notice" ("ASN").]

Conditions and Price Determination

This component enables one to store pricing stipulations agreed with the vendor (such as applicable discounts or surcharges, or stipulations regarding the payment of freight costs) in the system. One can enter these conditions in quotations, outline purchase agreements, and info records. For example, one also has the option of entering general conditions at the vendor level. The system then applies the conditions in determining the price in purchase orders (POs). There are three kinds of price in purchasing:

1. **Gross price:** Price without considering any possible discounts and surcharges.
2. **Net price:** Price that includes applicable discounts and surcharges.
3. **Effective price:** Net price after deduction of cash discount, with allowance for any miscellaneous provisions, delivery costs, and non-deductible taxes.

EXERCISES

1. What is the use of 'search key' required in item control module?
2. Distinguish between BoM and Formula Management module.
3. Explain the functionalities available in GL module in SAP.
4. Discuss the MPS procedure in detail with examples.
5. Explain the input–output relationships between MRP and CRP.
6. Discuss purchasing module of Mfg/Pro.

CHAPTER 6

ERP Implementation

INTRODUCTION

ERP implementations differ significantly with respect to their motivation and objectives. These differences significantly affect the overall scope, design, and approach to the ERP implementation.

The rationale for implementation varies between companies and provides an indication of the type of implementation envisaged. In a recent study, it was noted that firms provided six reasons for implementing an ERP. The chief reason was the need for a common IT platform. Other reasons included a desire for process improvement, data visibility, operating cost reductions, increased responsiveness to customers, and improvements in strategic decision-making. In fact, before the year 2000, several firms felt the need of ERP for Y2K compliance.

ERP is certainly acting as an impetus for the replacement of a mix of aging legacy systems with a common platform. This replacement of legacy systems with a common platform had become imperative for a number of reasons, mainly because mix of aging legacy systems had led to high cost support, and the firms expected business benefits such as process improvements and data visibility to result in cost reductions.

Another study, by Deloitte Consulting, of individuals from 62 companies found that motivations for an ERP implementation fell into two broad categories: a resolution of technological problems, and a vehicle for solving operational problems, such as uncompetitive business performance and ineffective business processes. It was recognized that the ERP implementation problem includes strategic, organization and technical dimensions. These differences in rationale will, to some extent, determine the type and scope of ERP implementation.

We now give one example to illustrate the above points. A construction company decided to implement an ERP prior to selling their business. The major aim was to add value to the company to make them more attractive to potential purchasers. This required them to undergo a process of significant BPR in order to transform themselves into occupants of a niche market in the construction industry. Thus the adoption of an ERP would underscore the unique way to address the business processes. By implication, the efforts required for implementation implies a significant adaptation of the ERP concept and modification of the existing processes.

IMPLEMENTATION APPROACH

It is expected that ERP will be implemented in *well reengineered and process based organization.* If the organization has not done it, then it is expected to be carried out during implementation.

Business Process Reengineering (BPR) is considered to be a powerful tool for reengineering and successful ERP implementation. BPR is defined by Hammer and Champy (1993) as

> The fundamental rethinking and radical redesign of business processes to bring about dramatic improvements in critical contemporary measures of performance, such as cost, quality, service, and speed.

One major thrust behind the business process reengineering philosophy is to fix the process before automating them. This means simply that an organization should redesign its business processes before applying automated information technology such as ERP. If done correctly, this would produce an increase in performance, not only through the streamlining of the process, but also an additional increase through the use of properly applied information technology.

The critical question facing the organizations is what to do first—should the processes be reengineered first and then improved processes be automated or select from "menu" of supposedly world class best practices offered by the ERP packages and avoid BPR altogether or reengineer them after implementing ERP.

BPR and ERP—Inseparable Twins or Chicken-Egg Paradox

Processes, organization, structure and information technology are the key components of BPR which automates business processes across the enterprise and provides an organization with a well-designed and well-managed information system. Organizations have two options:

- Reengineer business processes *before* implementing ERP
- Directly implement ERP and *avoid* reengineering

In the first option of reengineering business processes, before implementing ERP, the organization needs to analyze current processes, identify non-value adding activities, redesign the process to create value for the customer, and then develop, in-house applications or modify an ERP system package to suit the organizations requirements. According to this view, employees will develop a good sense of process orientation and ownership.

This would be a customized solution considering the organization's structure, culture, existing IT resources, employee needs and promises relatively less disruption to routine work during the change programmer. It is likely to have a high probability of implementation. But the reengineered process may not be the best in the class, as the organization may not have access to world-class research and best practices. Moreover, this may be the only chance to radically improve in the near future and going for less than the best may be a costly mistake. Also, developing an in-house application or implementing a modified ERP can take a lot of time.

The second option of implementing ERP package is to adopt ERP with minimum deviation from the standard settings. All the processes in a company should conform to the ERP model and the organization has to change its current work practices and switch over to what the ERP system offers. This approach of implementation offers a world-class efficient and effective process with built-in measures and controls, and is likely to be quickly installed (need not necessarily be quickly implemented fully). But if the employees do not have good understanding of their internal customer needs or current processes, or if these processes are not well defined and documented, then it is quite possible that while selecting the standard process from the ERP package, employees may not be able to perceive the difficulties likely to be encountered during the implementation stage. Employees would lack process ownership and orientation. Other than technical issues, issues like organization structure, culture, lack of involvement of people, etc. can lead to major implementation difficulties, and full benefits of standard ERP package may not be achieved. It may lead to a situation where the organization may have to again reengineer its processes. This could be a very costly mistake.

Theoretically, the third option of reengineering business processes *during* implementation of ERP also exists. It may sound to be the best option but, being an ideal situation, it does not seem to be a practical option and is likely to cause maximum disruption to existing work. It should not be forgotten that during BPR and ERP initiatives, routine work is still to be carried out and customers need to be served.

We can conclude from the above discussions that there are no right and easy answers for implementation issues. Each approach has its own pros and cons. Implementing ERP system and/or BPR is an organizational revolution process itself. The decision to embark upon BPR and/or ERP is a strategic decision and would largely depend on the policy of the organization on the time and resources it is willing to commit. Considering today's business dynamics, companies simply cannot afford to spend years implementing technology solutions even if they offer the promise of workflow improvements and bottom-line gains. For some businesses, a lengthy implementation offers enough time for competitors to overtake them, or at least threaten their market position. In addition, experience shows that a long drawn-out implementation increases the risk of project failure, impacts system functionality, and/or integration, and reduces both the management's commitment to the task and its confidence in the project team. Especially in complex environments that involve multiple interdependent processes, the disruption caused by a long implementation may reduce productivity and compromise customer service and delivery performance.

ELEMENTS OF IMPLEMENTATION METHODOLOGY

Assuming a decision on the BPR and ERP product has been taken, the implementation of ERP normally consists of five stages:

1. Design
2. Implementation
3. Stabilization
4. Continuous improvement
5. Transformation.

This structured implementation programme can speed system deployment and return on investment. This can be done in the following manner:

- Conducting an effective gap assessment
- Business and technical processes
- Organizational measures
- Data conversion and data clean-up
- Agreeing on the implementation boundaries
- Project sponsorship and governance.

The implementation strategy is ultimately built on a foundation of people, processes, and product as follows:

(i) People: This refers both to the people directly involved in the implementation, and the associated issues that crop up when a new tool appears on the scene. The challenge is to have a strong change management, organizational, and project management skills that will likely reduce risk and manage complexity. Successful team-building hinges on experienced leadership to evaluate and assemble the resources required—both internally and externally—to plan and launch a successful implementation and keep it on track. The best implementation teams represent a combination of business, process, and product knowledge; skill sets; and communication efforts—all of which encourage people to share information and responsibility for the project's success.

(ii) Process: To secure management commitment and ongoing support, it is necessary to define a business case for the ERP, focusing first on the core functionality that provides the best and fastest payback to achieve rapid implementation and return-on-investment, the successful implementation strategy should leverage the best practices built into the system, and processes should be realigned accordingly.

(iii) Product: The implementation partner should possess a thorough understanding of the capabilities and technical skills of the software tools to provide interfaces, and integration with other systems within the enterprise, and have business foresight to determine how the software can best be applied to further the organization's goals.

There are three commonly used ways of implementing ERP:

(i) The big bang: In this approach, which is the most ambitious and difficult of approaches to ERP implementation, companies cast off all their legacy systems at once and install a single ERP system across the entire company. Though this method dominated early ERP implementations, very few companies dare to attempt it anymore because it calls for the whole company to mobilize and change at once. Most of the ERP implementation failure stories from the late 1990s warn us about companies that used this strategy. Getting everyone to cooperate and accept a new software system at the same time requires tremendous effort, largely because the new system will not have any advocates. No one within the company has any experience using it, so no one is sure whether it will work.

(ii) Franchising strategy: This approach suits large or diversified companies that do not share many common processes across business units. Independent ERP systems are installed in each unit, while linking common processes such as financial bookkeeping, across the enterprise. This has emerged as the most common way of implementing ERP. In most cases, each business has its own "instances" of ERP, that is, a separate system and database. The systems link together only to share the information necessary for the corporation to get a large picture of its performance across all the business units (business unit revenues, for example), or for processes that don't vary much from business unit to business unit (perhaps HR benefits).

(iii) Slam-dunk: ERP dictates the process design in this method, where the focus is on just a few key processes, such as those contained in an ERP system's financial module. The slam-dunk is generally for smaller companies expecting to grow into ERP. The goal here is to get ERP up and running quickly and to ditch the fancy reengineering in favour of the ERP system's "canned" processes. Only a few companies that have approached ERP this way can claim much payback from the new system.

Some of the rules that are to be followed during implementation are as follows:

1. Linking business strategy with package selection and implementation.
2. Focusing on "vital" processes so as not to compromise on core areas.
3. Address the business system elements holistically, i.e. it is not sufficient to only address processes and IT during ERP, one has to look for what changes are required in organization structure, skills, employee KRA (Key Result Areas) and evaluation, policies relative to suppliers, customers, employees, business partners, and so on.
4. Using change management tools from the initial phases up to the final take-off. The user training must be planned in a proper way.
5. Adopting a tailored methodology to suit every situation. Every organization implementing ERP is in a unique situation, depending upon factors such as the status of ERP selection, objectives for ERP (replacing existing systems, automation or transformation), and complexity (which

depends upon the number of sites, culture, industry and others). Obviously, there's no "one-size-fits-all" when it comes to ERP implementation methodology.

6. Applying exacting criteria in choosing the implementation team which consists of both internal and external consultants.

Problems in ERP Implementation

Some of the major problems encountered while implementing ERP are as follows:

- The cost is likely to be underestimated.
- The time and effort to implement are likely to be underestimated.
- The resources from both the business and IT are likely to be higher than anticipated.
- The level of outside expertise required will be higher than anticipated.
- The changes required to business processes will be higher than expected.
- Scope control will be more difficult than expected.
- There will never be enough training, particularly across different modules.

Cost of ERP

The major costs of ERP implementation typically include:

Training: Training is the near-unanimous choice of experienced ERP implementers as the most underestimated budget item. Training expenses are high because workers almost invariably have to learn a new set of processes, not just a new software interface. Worse, outside training companies may not be able to help you. They are focused on telling people how to use software, not on educating people about the particular ways you do business. Prepare to develop a curriculum yourself, which identifies and explains the different business processes that will be affected by the ERP system.

Integration and testing: Testing the links between ERP packages and other corporate software links that have to be built on a case-by-case basis is another often-underestimated cost. A typical manufacturing company may have add-on applications—from the major e-commerce and supply chain to the minor sales tax computation and bar coding. All these require integration links to ERP. If you can buy add-ons from the ERP vendor, which are pre-integrated, you're better off. If you need to build the links yourself, expect things to get turn for the worse. As with training, testing ERP integration has to be done from a process-oriented perspective. Veterans recommend that instead of plugging in dummy data and moving it from one application to the other, run a real purchase order through the system, from order entry through shipping and receipt of payment—the whole order-to-cash banana—preferably with the participation of the employees who will eventually do those jobs.

Customization: Add-ons are only the beginning of the integration costs of ERP. Much more costly, and something to be avoided, if at all possible, is actual customization of the core ERP software itself. This happens when the ERP software can't handle one of your business processes and you decide to fiddle with the software to make it do what you want. This is dangerous. Customizations can affect every module of the ERP system because they are all so tightly linked together. Upgrading the ERP package—no walk in the park under the best of circumstances—becomes a nightmare because you'll have to do the customization all over again in the new version. May be it will work, may be it won't. No matter what, the vendor will not be there to support you. You will have to hire extra staff to do the customization work, and keep them on for good to maintain it.

Data conversion: It costs significantly to move corporate information, such as customer and supplier records, product design data, etc. from old systems to new ERP system. Most of the time it is observed that the data in the legacy system is of little use. Companies often deny their data is not clean until they actually have to move it to the new client/server set-ups that ERP packages require. Consequently, those companies are more likely to underestimate the cost of the move. But even clean data may demand some processing to match the ERP implementation requirements.

Data analysis: Often, the data from the ERP system must be combined with data from external systems for analysis purposes. Users with heavy analysis needs should include the cost of a data warehouse in the ERP budget. But refreshing all the ERP data every day in a big corporate data warehouse is difficult. ERP systems are normally not very efficient in indicating which information has changed from day to day, thus making selective warehouse updates tough. One expensive solution is custom programming. The company has to analyze all these costs before finalizing the deal.

Consultants' charges: Companies have to pay hefty fees to consultants for the process study, mapping and implementation. Hence care should be taken to identify objectives for which its consulting partners must aim when training internal staff. Typically, it may include the metrics in the consultants' contract for assessment of implementation performance.

Hiring correct people: It is an accepted fact that ERP success depends on staffing the project with the best and brightest people. The software is too complex, and it is necessary to have people with proper skills for the success of ERP implementation.

Steps in ERP Implementation

We will now discuss about the steps in ERP implementation methodologies. Various methodologies have been suggested by various ERP brands. For example, SAP suggests **ASAP,** Baan suggests **Target,** Oracle suggests **AIM,** Origin suggest **Implant** for QAD, Movex suggests **Implex**, and so on.

These techniques believe in leveraging a structured process to ensure consistent quality standards in every project. Some of the benefits of this approach are:

- Provides a rapid deployment environment for implementation
- Helps eliminate common errors in implementation
- Business process guide with detailed business process flow documentation mapped to particular ERP product's Applications and functionalities
- Configuration guide with detailed configuration documentation for each application module
- Data conversion and interface templates and design.

Normally these methodologies have the following phases:

Project planning and initiation: During the project planning and initiation phase, emphasis is placed on building a detailed and achievable work plan that establishes a balance between business drivers and efficiency. Establishing a well-defined implementation scope early in the project will give the team a common reference point and an effective way to communicate. It is also during this phase that the steering committee and program office will be established. The steering committee will be the final authority in approving scope changes, major changes in the project plan, and final Go/No-Go to production. In addition to any hardware setups, application products will be installed and patched to current release levels.

Business requirements definition: Business requirements definition will define the business needs that must be met by the implementation project. It is during this phase that business requirements will be mapped onto standard application functionality and gaps identified. As gaps between requirements and functionality emerge, they will be resolved by documenting workarounds, alternative solutions, or by changing the underlying business process. In an accelerated implementation approach, only standard Application functionality will be implemented. Any requirements that cannot be addressed with standard functionality will be addressed outside the scope of the implementation project.

Application configuration and solution design: During this phase, application set-ups will be completed. It is also at this time that the data conversion process will be defined in detail. The manual method is generally preferred due to its simplicity and the time constraints associated with an accelerated implementation approach. Project team members will also create detailed business procedure documentation. Supporting business requirements may require building application extensions to standard features. While new system designs are being finalized, the application and technical architecture begins to take form. The technical staff designs a technical architecture that can support the standard application configuration and customization.

Build and test business processes: If customizations, extensions, or conversions are required, they will be addressed during the *build phase.* Business system testing will be conducted through a series of conference room pilots. During the first pilot, basic application set-ups and functionality are tested. During the second pilot, converted or entered data, revised set-ups, and end-to-end business processes are tested. Participation in these activities by key finance users is essential, as it will provide them with valuable application experience, which is an essential part of their training.

Pre-production or transition: During the transition, the project team employs the new system in the client organization. The project team trains the users while the technical team configures the production environment and converts data. Also, during this phase users will perform the user acceptance test. The transition phase ends with the switchover to production when users start performing their job duties using the new system. The key users take on the task of training administrators and other members of the user community.

Production migration and support: During production migration, the project team will use the finished solution in the organization. The transition will be complete when data is converted, and end users have started to use the new system. When the system is stabilized, regular maintenance and system refinement can begin.

The deliverables in the above phases are the following:

1. Project work plan and schedule
2. Acceptance procedure
3. Change control procedure and logs
4. Defect reporting and tracking procedure and logs
5. Issue tracking procedure and logs
6. Status reports
7. Completed business requirement questionnaires
8. Installed and patched applications
9. Initial project environment, i.e. business requirements analysis
10. Business requirement scenarios
11. Reporting requirements
12. Audit and control requirements
13. Gap analysis
14. Design/Configure/Mapping
15. Application set-ups
16. Design documents
17. Build and testing including initialization of test environment
18. System test scripts for conference room pilots
19. Defect reports
20. Test summary report

21. Transition/Pre-Production/Training including initialization of training environment
22. Training plan and schedule
23. High level-module level user training documentation production migration
24. Transition strategy
25. Initialized production environment
26. Configured applications
27. Documented support procedure
28. Production ready system.

All the major ERP brands claim that they have a comprehensive, configurable methodology covering the entire project life cycle, from software selection, through implementation and system optimization. Typically, these are created from the knowledge gained in multiples of rollouts of implementation projects.

For example, Baan says "Target Enterprise has been used effectively by a broad spectrum of customers worldwide. Many years of experience have taught us how to develop and execute implementation plans that achieve the business objectives of our users' Baan project."

In fact, Baan has an implementing tool called *Dynamic Enterprise Modeler* which takes advantage of pre-built business reference models that define business processes and functions supported by Baan software. It has the steps and methods defined, which allow users to simulate all the activities to easily adapt the models to their own specific environment. The linking to the actual software and setting parameters makes it possible to deliver complete solutions at significantly reduced implementation times.

EXERCISES

1. Explain the critical role of BPR in ERP implementation.

2. Discuss the various steps in ERP implementation.

3. "Major cost of ERP is the implementation cost". Comment.

4. Explain DEM module in Baan.

5. Compare the implementation methodologies of different ERP brands.

PART II
MAKING ERP A SUCCESS

CHAPTER 7

ERP "As Is"

It is observed that any new management concept, when launched in India, reduces to *Indian Version*. ERP is not an exception to this rule. Hence we find JIT and Indian JIT, Single Sourcing and Indian Way of Single Sourcing, MRP and Indian MRP and also ERP and Indian ERP. In this chapter, let us discuss in detail the status (As Is) of *ERP in India* as *Indian ERP*.

CURRENT MARKET SCENARIO

The Express computer survey (2003) says that nine companies out of ten who have adopted ERP had disastrous experiences of its implementation. Many times during implementation they had to face a likelihood of the death of this ERP application. In fact, often the kind of chaos ERP implementation has created in this country, it looks as if only textile companies in India will use ERP as an *efficient tool* for negotiating the closing of their factories. The same scenario is seen even in blue chip industrial sectors like pharmaceuticals, food and automobiles, needless to mention the cement, textiles, tyre, and rubber industries.

Let us look at the number realities of ERP implementation status in India. Table 7.1 shows the overall adoption of ERP in India.

Table 7.1 Adoptions Status of ERP in India (%)

	Small (< 50 employees)	Medium (50–499 employees)	Large (> 500 employees)
Number of PC owning organizations who are aware of ERP across top 8 cities of India	45,029	16,572	4063
Implemented	0.9%	6.5%	35.6%
Planning/Evaluating	2.7%	4.7%	33.5%
Not considering seriously	81.5%	75.9%	28.8%
Refused to answer	14.7%	13.0%	2.1%

Source: IDC (India)

The report goes further to note a superstition that most of the companies carry (of course, before ERP Implementation) that *All you need to do to turn your business around is to plug in an ERP solution and bingo, all will be well.* But the real-life scenario is altogether different. To support this view, an instance is narrated of a 50 crore Delhi-based manufacturer of toiletries, who sought salvation from a popular ERP solution sold by a reputed vendor in mid-1998. Two years later, only a minuscule 2.4 percent of its overnight orders were being processed on the firm's expensive ERP application, and even that little bit of data was full of errors. The resultant chaos pushed the company perilously close to bankruptcy.

Similar failure stories of ERP implementations resulting from huge cost and time overruns and outright failures from all segments of corporate India abound, so much so that the Cassandras were out with predictions of the death of ERP.

A recent Gartner study (2001) found that the average cost overrun in Indian ERP implementations was 178 percent, the average implementation time overrun was 230 percent of original expectations, and the average decline in productivity was an astonishing 59 percent.

In this context, it is interesting to study the existing ERP players in India and their performance. Figure 7.1 shows the current (2003) market scenario in India. SAP India tops the charts with a 56 percent share followed by QAD at 10.8 per cent. Ramco at 10 percent, Baan at 8 percent, Oracle at 6 percent, PeopleSoft at 3.5 percent, J.D. Edwards at 3 percent, and ESS at 2.5 percent are the other major players. The remaining is compared mostly of the unorganized sector as well as ERP solutions developed in-house. In 2000, the Indian ERP market accounted for nearly 8.4 percent of the total Asia-Pacific market of system solutions amounting to Rs. 250 crore (IDC-2000).

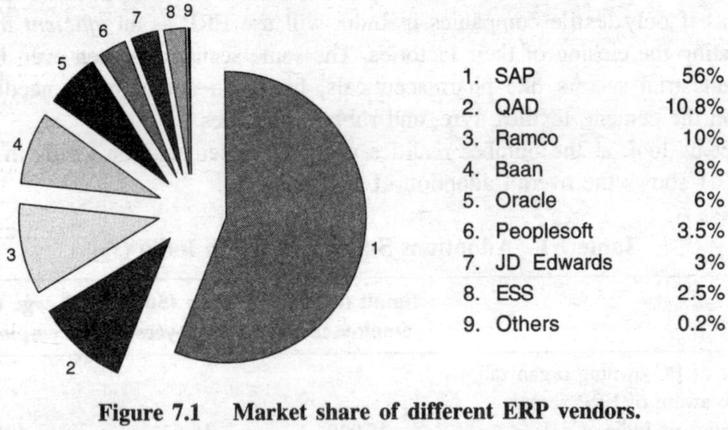

Figure 7.1 Market share of different ERP vendors.

We find a typical pattern of adoption of ERP culture in India. Manufacturing firms such as FMCG, automotive, steel, oil, textile, and pharmaceutical companies mainly use ERP dominating the overall picture. For these early adopters, Finance and Accounting, Sales and Distribution, Materials Management/Purchase, and Manufacturing are the most popular ERP modules implemented. In recent times,

Plant Maintenance, HR, Transportation, Service modules are growing in popularity. We find quite a long list of ERP installations such as TISCO, Tate Motors (TELCO), Nestle, Reliance, Godrej, Larsen & Toubro, Hindustan Lever Ltd. (HLL), and Maruti, which can be regarded as the prominent in the list of early adopters. The oil and gas companies including IOCL, HPCL, BPCL, ONGC, Shell, Essar, etc. and even some IT-savvy PSUs (Public Sector Units) such as ITI (Indian Telephone Industry), Konkan Railways, Delhi Metro, etc. are already listed as ERP sites. We find different industrial sectors like cement sector e.g. L & T cement, power sector, e.g. BSES (Bombay Suburban Electricity Supply), Food sector, e.g. Foodland are going for ERP solutions. The construction or project companies, e.g. Gammon and Shapoorji Palanaji, have also implemented different (not greatly branded) ERP solutions suitable to their needs, whereas HCC (Hindustan Construction Company) had developed a customized ERP catering to their requirements.

Though direct vendors like SAP, Mfg/Pro, Baan, etc. dominate the ERP space in India, a recent trend that has added impetus to the market is the emergence of ERP consultants who are third-party providers who not only implement the vendor solutions at client sites, but also provide maintenance as well as implementation services. For example, *Thirdware Solutions*, one such third-party provider for implementation of QAD Mfg/Pro solutions had implemented Mfg/Pro at Ford Motor Company, Delphi Automotive, Lear Seating, Tata Johnson Controls, HLL, Godrej Soaps, Fosters India, Bacardi India, Dabur India, Sara Lee, Pilsbury, Nicholas Piramal, Allen Bradley, Raychem RPG, Tata Liebert, Schlumberger and GE Lighting. Siemens Information Systems (SISL) is another major third-party player involved in implementing Baan, SAP and even Oracle solutions. SISL has around 70 implementations, some major clients being Marico Industries, Hero Honda, Sanmar Engineering, Chemplast, Osram and Novartis. PeopleSoft solutions are being implemented by Chennai-based Hexaware Technologies.

Currently, the SME segment in India has been one of the most aggressive adopters of ERP software. In fact, of the 791 firms in India today having an ERP, almost 60 percent belong to the SME segment. This substantial increase in the penetration level in the SME segment is attributed to the different vendors coming out with country-specific localizations (providing solution to legalities), availability of large pool of skilled functional and technical talent, and significant dropping in the total cost of ownership of an ERP.

Some of the prominent names in the SME segment include Tribhovandas Bhimji Zhaveri, Nippo Batteries, Baroda Dairy, and Haldiram Among the vendors active in the SME segment is ESS which has pioneered solutions specific to SME firms. The Rs. 260 crore Indo-National, best known for its Nippo brand of batteries, is a typical example of an ESS implementation. ESS has implemented its flagship product called *ebizframe* to automate their Corporate Office in Chennai as well as their branch offices and two factory locations in Tada and Nellore. The primal objectives that the company has for switching to ERP is to get aid in smooth inventory management, timely scheduling of production cycles and shipment of goods, managing human resources and online data communication.

Interestingly, according to IDC estimates, the ERP market in India has been witnessing a CAGR of 70 percent over the last 5-6 years. As a result, the market has leapfrogged over the years from Rs. 12 crores in 1995-96, Rs. 27 crores in 1996-97, Rs. 62 crores in 1997-98, Rs. 134 crores in 1998-99, Rs. 250 crores in 1999-2000, to Rs. 460 crores in 2000-2001. The recent report says that the ERP market will touch 507.5 crores by 2005-2006. Thus the picture looks rosy for the ERP market.

Claimed Tangible Benefits

The IDC report underlined the tangible quantitative benefits accrued by Indian companies in post-ERP implementation era. According to the report, BPCL claims that it has worked on the ROI on SAP R/3 implementation, totalling Rs. 40 crores on annual savings. Fosters India claims, "In the absence of an ERP solution (MFG/PRO from QAD), closing of our accounts would take more than 20 days, but now it takes less than a week."

According to the Konkan Railways, "Our in-house ERP called RMS helped us make substantial savings and now the other railways also intend to purchase the application from us." On the other hand, ERP companies like SAP India claims: "Our list of successful ERP implementations include BPCL, IOCL, ONGC, Reliance, Coca Cola, Pepsi, ITC, Colgate-Palmolive, Procter & Gamble, Mahindra & Mahindra and TELCO. All these companies are using our R/3 ERP application."

In general, we find such remarks published and marketed across the country. Most of the time these benefits are difficult to prove on statistical grounds as soft benefits like comfort in work life, maturity in planning, attitude changes, transparency, visibility, etc. are either practically impossible to measure or correlate such improvements to ERP implementation. Companies are supposed to set their objectives prior to implementation followed by measuring of the achievements after implementation, and only then should they conclude about the effects of ERP. Unfortunately, it is observed that clear and measurable objectives are not at all set and updated, but some document called 'scope and boundary' does exist, which is normally used for *phase-wise payment* to consultants. The scenario could be better for some companies where meticulous assessment is made; but again, those cases are not enough in numbers to make the overall average improved.

Implementation Realities

In one of the corporate training programmes on ERP, the author was asked to name one Indian company which is 100 percent satisfied with ERP implementation, however, no convincing answer to this has yet been found.

Satisfaction could be attributed by fulfillment of one simple expectation that the company is using *only one* ERP system for *all* the transactions happening day in and out. This typically must include proper planning of salaries of employees, taxes, cash purchases, maintenances of machineries, annual maintenance contract' of gardening, payment scheduling to security service provider, consultants payments, spare parts consumption, annual gathering expenses, etc., along with complete manufacturing planning, sales planning, engineering and design planning, and so on. In reality, we always find at least one more system (could be manual also) is being used along with the main ERP system to accommodate some transactions that may be possibly addressed through ERP. Unfortunately, sometimes this one more system is *another ERP*. That means, after investing crores of rupees in ERP implementation, companies are still dissatisfied or looking for ways to improve existing implementation status. Sometimes it happens under the name of ERP-II adoption or Supply Chain solutions, or simply enhancements of existing ERP, which can be really construed as *organized way of going wrong with confidence*. This happens because of some weird calculations and supporting strategy.

The following are the myths prevailing around ERP, which summarize its exact status of conceptual understanding in India:

1. ERP is nothing but *everyday reduction of profit or early risky proposition.*
2. There are different concepts of ERP based on ERP vendors.
3. ERP is computerization project of the company.
4. ERP is a software system.
5. ERP is advanced legacy system.
6. ERP modules are individually ERP solution.
7. ERP in India must be *Indian ERP.*
8. Customized ERP is ERP.
9. ERP is outdated now and ERP II is the right solution.
10. ERP is a downsizing tool.
11. ERP is applicable to only manufacturing set-ups and not for service sectors.
12. ERP is the panacea to all business problems.
13. ERP only supports transactional needs.
14. ERP is a white elephant.
15. ERP is a fad and has already gone away.
16. More the number of ERP systems you have, the more productivity you get.
17. ERP is not suitable to small scale companies due to costs and implementation time.

We see here that the width of misunderstandings regarding ERP ranges from black magic to total omnipotence. The scenario can be metaphorically described as water, water everywhere and not a drop to drink. The reasons behind this scene could be classified into two groups. The first set includes the marketing efforts of ERP vendors portraying that ERP is everything and, on the other hand, the second set includes those who give bad publicity to ERP.

We will now examine various issues related to ERP implementation in the Indian context.

The Indian Scenario

It will not be an exaggeration to comment that the more you get implementation experience of ERP across the globe (especially USA), the more you become *unsuitable* to understand Indian companies. This happens because of innumerable reasons, especially reasons such as deviations in volumes of transactions, varied culture, IT understanding, expectations and needs, discipline, the approach adopted infrastructure, overall ERP suitability, etc. as also the type of consulting available in the country. It does not mean that ERP software designed and developed out of India cannot be suitable to India because sometimes, ERP software developed in India is also found not suitable for Indian companies.

The fundamental question behind the ERP suitability is the *readiness status for ERP* in the Indian context itself. Are we really matured for an ERP culture? In fact, talking of some sectors like cement, heavy engineering, textiles, foundries etc., are we really matured for any integrated computerized systems at all? Most of the time the answers are not that encouraging. Another way to this problem is to improve right away from the legacy systems (e.g. manual cardex system) to sophisticated ERP system by **business process reengineering**. This is what is happening in India and is also the reason why ERP is not rated very successful in India.

BPR (Business Process Reengineering) is a double-edged tool: when not applied properly, it will destroy the user first. By its very concept, BPR is demanding too much from the Indians today. It asks for absolute change in the mindset and supports only analytical and logical thinking. Managing business in India is more tricky than analytical, and has more illogical (sometimes these can also be referred as **creative**) transactions than the disciplined ones. Since BPR cannot support such transactions, ERP cannot address those issues and we see ERP failures happening around. In fact, the overall exercise of carrying BPR in India itself generated (**degenerated** actually) version of **Indian BPR** where process improvements are ignored and heavy functional automations are sought of, and where ERP has exposed its limitations to integrate such absurd requirements. Hence we see that typical Indian requirements are not at all addressed by ERP. For example, the marketing executive demands access to purchase module because he also buys promotion materials and expects ERP to automatically generate Purchase Order without rates, without supplier, and also without item codes. This is just because the user wants PO number to get advance money and proceed for actual purchasing, and is really not sure of what he is buying till the moment he pays for it. Indian BPR will promote (or will not strongly and successfully resist) such requirements by *customizing* ERP. Over a period of time, with such pieces of customization, ERP becomes Indian ERP. In fact, users will claim later that the old manual system was more efficient, effective and also economical as compared to new Indian ERP. Unfortunately, most of the time they are correct in saying so.

Secondly, in most of the Indian ERP implementation cases, companies have to start from very basic initiatives of introductory computer training and then climb the ladders of transactional automation and further seamless planning of all the resources. The kind of resistance received at every phase will create hindrances of ERP success and increase in geometric proportion. If the consulting efforts fall short at any moment, the whole project will ultimately result in chaos.

Thirdly, we see that the marketing team of ERP vendors gives any member of *assurances* for obvious reasons. Later, the poor implementation team has to cope with the unrealistic expectations of users during implementation. This normally hampers the morale and motivation of consultants as well as the users, and ultimately results in temporary patch works than permanent process improvement solution. Also, it will *expedite* the turnover of consultants from one place to another and create further frustrations in users as they have to now restart the whole process of updating functional requirements for new consultants.

The study of ERP implementation in more than 65 organizations in India reveals the various eye-opening realities and root causes of improper methodologies followed right from ERP vendor selection to user training. We will now discuss this aspect in various Indian industrial sectors.

FEATURES OF FULL CYCLE INDIAN ERP IMPLEMENTATION

The normal process of ERP adoption in the big Indian companies starts in the executive class of the airplane. The MD of the client company incidentally meets the Marketing Chief of X brand ERP vendor there. Then the discussion takes (especially at 40,000 ft from earth's surface), more or less on recent IT trends in the world and then the focus shifts to the Indian scenario. Ultimately, the term 'ERP' is introduced to the MD as a **solution** to his business problems. The information is provided regarding ERP is of such a *quality* that the MD immediately attains the 'supreme level of understanding' of ERP and also regrets for not having such a solution in the company so far. He is also provided with sensitive piece of information in respect of his competitor company's recent (or may be older) decision of going for X ERP brand. The MD now well understands why he makes losses, why competitors are ahead of him, why his manufacturing is below standards, why distribution is less productive, why inventories are huge, why employees are unhappy, and also why his son is not getting married. The answer to all these is not having ERP in place.

The next meeting of the ERP vendor with the MD conveniently takes place preferably with EDP (Electronic Data Processing) Head and other top managers from the client's side, and the decision officially gets declared that the company is now going for X ERP implementation. They also set objectives and create scope and boundary document for the overall ERP project. While making such a document the vendor helps them in copying most of the things from another similar document prepared for some other company. Having done all these, the company has the following understanding about ERP:

- The MD is now assured of huge profits in the coming financial years.
- Prudent VPs (Vice Presidents) recommend one more job role of Chief Information Officer (CIO) in the company with all perquisites applicable to the President and the CEO.

- The EDP Manager is now sure of his job as one project will be on.
- Others in the EDP are happy to get trained on ERP free of cost, i.e. without any monetary investment, which otherwise would have cost them heavily.
- The Marketing Head is of a mixed opinion, not quite sure how ERP will reduce inventory (because he is very much sure of his *contributions* in building inventory), but is more or less sure on the removal of one major complaint normally put forth by his marketing team that their performance is lower because the competitor has ERP.
- Other functional heads like Manufacturing, Quality, Design, Planning or Purchase etc. are indifferent to the decision except for saying yes. In fact, the Maintenance Head is not even called for this exercise and learns from reliable sources that something related to computerization is planned in the company and perhaps it will create job damages to all those who are involved. He takes his usual spanner and is now happy that he was not even called for the event.
- The political tussle starts now on the selection issue of the internal implementation team. Everybody (in the middle management) is aware of potential marketability of ERP consulting, and the best way left is to switch carrier from hard core functional (thankless) job to comfortable IT job. In some industries, we also find a common trend of registering for courses like, C, C++, or Oracle, Developer 2000 etc., to put the candidature properly.
- The rest of the people including supervisors, workers, trainees, and others ignore the news as they had seen the ISO 9000 project or the TQM project. In fact, they are very much sure about the overall failure of the ERP project within the estimated timeframe.
- There exists one small group from all the levels of the organization, which is really impressed by the concept and excited about the extraordinary results expected.

The internal cross-functional implementation team is then formed. The external consulting has already been awarded to a reputed consulting firm based on its **brand name** and the level of implementation experience in the same industry. In reality, though, the consulting firm has implemented ERP in a similar industry, the fact remains that they have already lost those consulting resources to another consulting firm. However, the client does not seem to have interest in such issues and happily awards the contract. Finally, one fine morning, by traditionally breaking the coconut, the implementation starts.

Most of the reputed ERP brands have their own implementation methodology; accordingly, consultants start training of internal implementation team. Needless to say, the training typically includes information sharing in *power point presentation* about X brand ERP, its flexibilities, strengths, successful installations, and then practical screen based training is done. Then the so-called 'As Is' business study is carried out and 'To Be' refined processes are recommended. The real challenge now is to involve users and start master data loading into the system.

The ERP systems have the following major masters to be filled in:

- Company Masters
- Item Master
- Bill of Materials or Formula Master
- Machine Master
- Routing Master
- Store Master
- Customer Master
- Supplier Master
- Accounts Master

The prime factor in ERP implementation is the proper and complete entries in these masters. But normally, users, while furnishing information regarding masters, hardly realize that the success of ERP is the direct function of quality of master entry. They tend to give *judgments with safety factor added* than scientifically calculated figures. A simple rule then is observed as "Garbage in is garbage out" (GIGO), which can explain the low levels of outputs generated through ERP systems. Such instances are very common in most of the Indian companies today.

These master entries are somehow validated and the next job of *parallel run* starts. Here, users are expected to work in ERP as well as in their regular legacy system. A lot of problems and frustrations could be observed and felt during this phase. Some of these issues are given in detail in the subsequent discussion. Finally, after some *deadline*, the organization decides to live with ERP. Most of the Indian companies love 1st January (12 cases), or 1st July (18 cases) or 1st October (16 cases) as go live days. This deadline many a time gets postponed and ultimately *dies* one day. The very next issue then will be neither the old system available nor the new system. The sad scenario then includes sometimes going back to the old systems, or adding one more system over ERP, or continuing with ERP with a very low morale. Just as luck would have it, the problem gets aggravated when the external consultants run away from the site. The whole and sole responsibility now comes on the internal consulting team, whatever is remaining of it. Many of them have already left jobs or are in the process of leaving to start implementing X brand of ERP *successfully* elsewhere. Now the organization (if lucky) starts managing its ERP with whatever handful of people it has, and is somehow able to print purchase requisitions, sale orders, etc. through the ERP system. In fact, this is called *successful implementation*. Once users along with consultants attempt to run MRP, RCCP, and also to some extent DRP, after looking at the pathetic results and recommendations generated, they never even look at those menus again. Similarly, the forecasting module will be ignored. Production orders generated after physical production, spare parts requirement comes manually, inventory valuation taken place separately in finance module, and to the extent that every planning is done in Excel work sheets. The worst part is that these excel outputs are imported in ERP; in fact, some smart IT companies provide *software interfaces* for data uploading from Excel to ERP databases. Some companies resort to manual entries and reporting because those are found economical and efficient as compared to ERP.

Most of the functional heads now insist on two types of information, one is what the ERP gives, and the other what is the actual status. Users find their own ways to tackle these whimsical demands. Therefore, ERP becomes on line but reflects information that is four days back.

Thus ERP at its own pace gets *stabilized* with routine complaints and arguments. The organization still continues with its usual profit (or loss) making and, slowly, everybody recovers from the ERP fever. Now they are in a better position to focus on their day-to-day performance rather than talking and fighting on something called ERP.

One fine morning the same Marketing Chief of X ERP brand (or different this time) meets the MD again. The MD, being wiser now, blasts him. The Marketing Chief, being thick skinned, takes everything lightly and asks the same question to MD which he had asked a few months back: why does he make losses, why his competitors are ahead of him, why his manufacturing is below standards, why is the distribution less productive, why are the inventories so huge, why are the employees unhappy, and also why his son is yet to get married. This time the answer to all these is not 'not having ERP in place' but *only* ERP in place, or "lack of optimizing systems, i.e. lack of supply chain solution sitting top on ERP". The MD thinks for a while, slowly gets into the trap, and one day announces that the company is now going in for supply chain optimization to enhance global performance. He now has major concerns of what is to be done with the existing ERP, ERP trained people, and budget for SCM solution and consulting. Also, he has already seen the performance of external ERP consulting. With this background, he announces one more *great* decision. The company is now starting an IT division and all the IT solution implementation will be done through the new IT company. People from the parent organization are poached officially along with a few new ones. The SCM project now starts to sit on top of failed ERP.

This completes the full implementation cycle of Indian ERP. The cycle starts from one point and ends at the same point. The organization starts from non-efficient manual systems, goes through ERP, and ultimately returns to human tampered highly sophisticated optimizing supply chain solution. In fact, the company starts from **As Is** and returns to As Is. In the process, it learns that computers cannot replace humans.

WHY ERP IS 'AS IS'?

Let us now analyze a few cases of implementation problems and their unsuccessful elimination, which causes ERP status *As Is*. These observations are representative and attempts are made to give a feel of actual ERP implementation issues in India, which are generated by the clients and the consultants.

"I Can Leave My Soul But Not the Codification System"

The first and the foremost data about a company is the item data. We can see by the volume that the items are contributing to more than 85% of the resources in most of the manufacturing set-ups. The first information about the item is its code. In most of the companies there exists a typical item codification system, which is based on the logic of numbering. Their first few digits indicate something and then the next few indicate something different and, finally, the running serial number. Plossl (1994) advised way back in 1975 to give up such systems in MRP environment itself and advocated non-significant system of coding having continuous serial number. The need of significant coding system was felt because of the absence of sophisticated IT system in classical inventory control era. In fact, whatever significance is attached to numbers in different digits is well captured in item properties itself by MRP or ERP systems. Practically nobody in the organization knows exactly what is MRP, then forget Plossl and his advice. (Surprisingly, the author also comes across many ERP consultants who are not aware of APICS.)

The user strongly insists on continuation of the existing item-coding system and asks for *automation* of such things in ERP. He asserts that his existing FoxBASE or Cobol based system provides him with such requirements.

Earlier, popular ERP products were not supporting these needs (they used to support prefix or suffix to the numbers but not the different series or logic) and conflict now arises on this issue between the users and the consultants. The user is quite sure that if he loses his item-coding system, he will not be able to perform, a single routine job. In fact, in one reputed machine manufacturing company, the Head Engineering had conceptualized the significant coding system and showing the limitations of the coding system, was understood as exposing his own personal limitations. Consultants in such cases observed taking the backseat to accommodate significant coding without automation. In the whole process, considerable potential benefits resulting from reduced time for new item codification and item retrieving time retrieving time is lost. The same is also applicable to the PO number series, cost center series, SO number series, production order series, voucher series, etc.

Today, ERP vendors have come up with **number system module** where automatic generation of any series of significant coding can be handled. Incorporation of such facilities in ERP is the classic example of selling efforts of ERP vendors rather than accepting implementation challenges for overall benefits to the clients.

"I Don't Know"

In one textile company, the practice is to procure the packing materials from the sub-contractor, by providing raw materials from another supplier. In this case we find that the exact bill of materials is neither known to the company nor to the subcontractor. In fact, so many years the corrugated boxes were manufactured based on **general guidelines,** and not on accurate accounting principles. When it was to load BoM information into ERP, the company adopted the same practice of approximation rather than changing to proper BoM structuring. It had created total loss of on-hand inventory and cost information. Actually, this also amounts to a loss of everything that ERP brings in.

Secondly, when it goes to various lead times, such as purchase lead time of an item, manufacturing lead time of an item, etc., we get *standard* figures of 8 days, 3 months, 20 hours, etc. suggested by the users. These figures are more judgments than realities. The correct figures are either really not available or not shared with ERP masters. We can also find that the internal lead-time is of considerable amount as compared to external, and not at all accounted for. The main impact of such fallacious entries is *bullwhip effect* in planning, and hence ERP fails in providing proper planning recommendations.

When it comes to material ordering most of the Indian companies state that the tax on basic material cost is "As Applicable". The common approach in putting such remark on the PO (Purchase Order) also shows that the culture of *buyer* is completely missing in the organization. The last point of knowing the total material cost in ERP is just before taking material receipt entry. Even at that point also, companies are not sure of freight, loading unloading charges, turnover taxes, etc. Now the issue of proper material accounting starts between the user and the consultant. If the material receipt entry is passed on to ERP, it will calculate the inventory costs also and then there is no room for further ***revaluation*** of these lots again. For accounting purposes, the organization tends to settle such issues through debit-credit notes, which will not have effects on material accounting as such. Normally, in the Indian scenario such debit-credit negotiations run for months together, and they surpass all constraints of limit of financial years. The author has seen in one company the purchaser settled one such negotiation after nearly two years from material receipt transaction and the cost difference was Rs. 20. The cost of keeping such issue pending along with paper and system cost was much more than what was received, but the purchaser was appreciated for his efforts. In general, the approach of purchaser is "I don't know what I buy, in what quantity, what size of goods, from which location of supplier, and also at what rate I should buy." The poor ERP system in these cases is reduced to the costlier and sophisticated FoxBASE system.

Most of the time we find that the material comes in store without PO mentioned on the challan. Such cases occur because either the PO does not exist, or the supplier has not mentioned it on the challan. In the case of *blanket* PO, it is a common observation that no order is released promptly. In such case, store person cannot take receipt of the material immediately, which will lead to loss of on-hand inventory information. Though every organization is putting a lot of the so-called disciplinary verdicts, today still we are not able to resolve these issues. In every month, GM (Materials) declares "henceforth no receipts to be taken unless there exist a PO number on the challan". The very next day *urgent* material comes in with his instructions over telephone, and it does not even has a purchase requisition. Then the organization suddenly realizes that *we are not for ERP but ERP is for us.* ERP should have *flexibility* to address these requirements. In some cases where the item is new and does not have any code, the purchaser buys the item in a hurry because of the pressure from demand side. When ERP does not allow taking receipt of such an item, a common argument that we can hear is

"Bringing material is my function and not waiting for system to create code for it." Though it sounds logical, no attempts are made to eliminate such instances by cross-functional joint efforts.

In one of the heavy engineering companies, the author came across the 'great' system of material issue. The store department did not know exactly to whom and for what (account) the issues are made. The maintenance department was the material receiver on behalf of other user departments and, till the moment they actually used the spares for a particular machine, they did not know against what it was to be charged. Consultants suggested various ways to address these requirements and overcome the current bad practices. But the users were fighting on the subject that no *additional* entry work should be passed on to them. Ultimately, the existing practice was *automated* and the valuable information of cost center accounting in real time was lost. The loss was to the extent that the practice of buying from revenue account and issuing to capital account seemed to be prevalent in ERP.

One more interesting phenomenon was observed in the case of import purchases. The user contends that different formats of import purchase are required because of varying needs of accommodations of import terms and conditions. The real issue is not the varying needs but *inconsistency* in accommodation of terms and conditions. The user sometimes selects one term for one item and the next time a different term even though the supplier is the same. Due to this non-standardization, ERP cannot be fully utilized and the user has to resort to either manual or some legacy system. Actually, this is not the functional requirement, but poor negotiating skills of the purchaser to settle transactions with least possible variations and bring more standardizations.

In project purchases we hardly find any discipline in India. The project engineer normally buys *systems* such as boilers, etc., and not the item as such. His arguments are "I don't know what is the individual cost of components, or even which components reach me through boiler as items."

The same argument he makes regarding the payment terms. He is not sure in what way he should confirm that all the purchased items are received in the stores and he can release payments. The basic cause of all these issues is lack of knowledge besides lack of interest in gaining knowledge.

With this background, it will not be a false statement if we say that in India less important things are tightly controlled and valuable things are least controlled. To support this, we can see one instance of a leading pharmaceutical company where the user insisted on separate *scrap module* in ERP to address scrap inventory issues like opening balance, closing balance, approval note, etc. In fact, he had classified scrap materials meticulously as project leftovers, repairs, sludge, production scrap, obsolete items, rejected items, and job work returns. He wanted visibility on scrap but did not know the basic rate of the project items that he was buying. ERP, if used in such environment, becomes *scrap* in the true sense as it is used only for scrap.

ERP Demands More Entries Than Manual System

In one of the cement manufacturing companies, the author came across another 'grand' system of material identification. The method was based on the logic that only one supplier supplies an item once in a year and hence no physical tagging as well as material accounting is necessary. The idea of *lot control* is the description of the item itself. The store authorities were asking to address such things in ERP where every entry of an incoming item cannot be skipped just because it is happening once in a year. When he was asked to enter the item details, a spontaneous comment was "in ERP we are doing more entries than previous manual system".

A similar instance was observed in one of the textile companies. They used to receive daily 80 tankers of water for the processing department. The manual inventory system was a Water Register wherein the quantity, PO number, supplier, etc. were recorded along with the tanker number (vehicle number). The users were entering those details per tanker and used to skip the repetitive detail by ticking 'as follows' for the remaining tankers. In fact, the whole register was specially printed for bringing such convenience of 'as follows'. When ERP demanded to make entry of each tanker to track tankerwise receipts, or suggested alternatively to make one entry of full quantity of all tankers, ignoring tankerwise information, it was observed that neither of the options were suitable to user's requirements. The user condemned both the alternatives as to be either time consuming or incomplete. Consultants did some automation to resolve these issues, which later caused serious bug in the main material receipt menu of ERP. In fact, the consultants should have taken the basic approach of challenging *information flooding* and restricted the users from doing useless entries. Ironically, tanker-wise entries were observed parallely made at the office gate register by security guards of the company (fortunately, office gate requirements were not within the ERP scope and boundary document).

Another typical problem which we find is the project material issues. Normally, the maintenance department requires various pipes and asks the basic measure of unit as meters, whereas the stores department prefers number as the basic unit of measure for material issues. Though ERP is capable of handling multiple units of measures, it requires a formula to convert these units of measures into one reference measure of unit. Regarding numbers to meters, we can have a constant formula if we issue standard meters per standard number. It never happened and actually the store cuts the pipe and gives the required meters to the maintenance department. To address this problem in ERP, we have to maintain entries per meter of material issue and also per number of material issue. The user becomes furious because, whenever a transaction takes place, he has to pass multiple entries.

We find a few interesting cases in the Indian oil sector. Purchasers buy various commodities from a number of suppliers, for which *open indent* is used, which the user departments generate. The quantities in open indent are based on the budget for that item set by the user department. The schedule of buying depends upon the *urgency* of the user and his communication with the purchaser. Most of the time we find that different user departments require the same item. Ideally, the store or materials department should plan such item, but it never happens in practice. In an ERP environment, the purchaser expects *control* on these repetitive transactions in terms of smooth scheduling and proper service level to users, whereas users want budget information vis-à-vis their demand pattern as also the consumption pattern. Functionally, the requirements very well qualify as genuine necessities, and ERP can help beyond expectations. But this will be true only if the planning discipline is maintained. All the requirements are to be routed either through MRP or through statistical model rather than generating one blanket requisition. Users now complain about the increase in work due to ERP, as they have to create more and more requisitions than in the past.

In general, many Indian companies feel that generating purchase requisitions is an additional workload caused by ERP. The legacy system allows anything to be bought without any reference of requisitions, or such reference could be built after the transactions. ERP, however, never allows such malpractice and always demands a proper procedure of material buying, which in a way is seen as *rigid* control.

In one food manufacturing company, the author came across some very hard arguments and resistance to pass entries, just because the users were not using the information generated out of those entries. Such cases prove the overall mentality of an organization and the lack of understanding of the ERP concept. The user department was the production department and consultants recommended to pass actual material issues entries against production orders. The earlier practice of the organization was to report production consumption at the store issue level, and later adjustments were done by the costing department by physical counting of unused material lying on the production floor. ERP practice suggested to transfer stock to production instead of consumption and production may *back flush* the materials, thus generating exact figures of costs and quantities. Production users including GM-Manufacturing resisted the idea of passing the required entries in ERP just because his staff were not having time for such matters; secondly, it was useless for him, and thirdly, he was not willing to do the costing job because the costing department already existed. Ultimately he agreed to pass these entries but with one data entry operator working for him. Today also, the production people look at entry work in ERP as third grade clerical task and never think of the reports it generates from this type of work.

"We Want Flexibility"

A very common complaint against ERP is its rigid structure and disciplined standard operating procedures (SOP). In fact, the successful performance of ERP is directly proportional to the adherence to SOP. We find ridiculous demands and expectations from users, which are conflicting with SOP. Hence ERP is either blamed or made to fail. When the user says he wants *flexibility* in ERP, actually he wants the official allowance to deviate from standards set for value generation. The repercussions of such flexibility are tremendous, including the loss of value.

In one garment manufacturing company, the author came across a typical style of customer negotiations. The sales people arbitrarily fixed unit price and raised sales orders against customers. After physical material dispatches, suddenly the customer started negotiating with sales and the rates were changed. The sales person then wanted to pass these entries in ERP. No good system will support such incongruous requirements. Here, the user wants flexibility in addressing these issues from ERP and also expected that everything should happen *automatically*. To settle and account for such changes, one has to pass a number of *reverse entries* in ERP. Eventually, the sales person will use ERP throughout his life.

Unfortunately, we find consulting companies in India charge extra from clients for automating such absurd provisions. The same thing happened in this company also and they landed up with *auto reverse entry module* supporting the existing system. More ironically, this feature of ERP soon became so popular that the company asked a similar module for purchase transactions. The ultimate chaos is always observed in finance and costing modules where we find multiple figures of profits, inventory values, sales income, taxes, etc. linked to the same transaction. Nobody could really gather any meaningful information from such sets of data over a period of time. The user gets flexibility and the organization gets punishment.

In one heavy machine manufacturing company, the author had seen flexibility requirements going to the extent of unethical business practices and in such cases illegal transactions. Unfortunately, all these were happening through a world class ERP product. The company was into heavy moulding machine manufacturing and the scenario is more or less make to order. The sales process normally initiates with preliminary discussions on the specifications of the machine, then *tentative* freezing of the requirements, and quoting of the price. Manufacturing planning starts once the acceptance of the sales order from the customer side is received. During manufacturing or even after completion of the product, suddenly the sales department realizes that the customer is no more *eligible* to receive the delivery. This could happen due to many factors, e.g., the customer fails to pay in time, the customer cancels his order, and sometimes customer asks for more facilitation such that the existing product cannot be improved. Sometimes the sales department finds more interesting (eligible) customer etc. Now the requirement is to change the ownership of all the activities that have happened so far to another customer, or simply to halt further value additions. In some cases the dismantling of existing assemblies is also required. Accordingly all the financial transactions have to be settled.

Many a time complexities are involved because the customer has paid advance and asks for refund, or a new customer demands different product configurations. The author has seen such diverted product gets diverted many times during its engineering stage up to dispatch stage (in fact, once after preparation of the excise gate pass, sales head directed the delivery to another customer). MRP runs in such cases take a toss and get blamed for impractical solution to this industry. Shop floor control or production orders are hardly respected and everything is tampered manually. Looking at the number of items (typically it includes more than 25 major assemblies, 300 subassemblies, and approximately 28,000 components) the user now expects to get *regularized* all these nonsense transactions through ERP and, moreover, ERP should provide with *suitable* reports on these transactions. The height of expectations could be seen when the user demands excise gate pass details should not tally with the sales order details, including customer name, because during transit anything may happen regarding the ownership title of the machine product. The standard ERP package cannot fit into such demand sizes unless one tears ERP into pieces and then stitches.

One peculiar requirement was once observed from a user of an automobile company. He asked for various options of selecting report sizes (A3 or A4) to use with different printers for printing the same reports. ERP was expected to be flexible enough to accommodate multiple report sizes based on printer selection. The same user never used in his earlier tenure any computerized output and did not even know how to load paper into printer.

We find such instances regarding the accommodation of price discounts, penalty clauses or promotional terms of trade in ERP. Virtually we find numerous *ideas* of *creative* heads of companies departments when they deal with selling or buying anything. Table 7.2 gives an idea of the same, which is observed in one bicycle manufacturing company in India.

Table 7.2 Terms Used in Sales Order

Penalty term	Type of customer	Type of product	Place of dispatch	Penalty percentage on sales value
Delay after credit days up to first 8 days	A	A	A	X1
	B	B	B	Y1
	C	C	C	Z1
Delay for the next one month	A	A	A	X2
	B	B	B	Y2
	C	C	C	Z2
Delay after one month	A	A	A	X3
	B	B	B	Y3
	C	C	C	Z3

Approximately 81 different permutations of penalty clauses were observed before ERP implementation in this company. Such practice was to be addressed even in ERP. Fortunately, the project head from client side was sensible and ERP was saved from doing all these.

The same thing can be observed in purchase orders also. When it comes to supplier selection and discounts, the purchaser is excited to show his skills in defining various complex terms and then land up with manual monitoring of such in ERP environment. An example from project item purchases is given in Table 7.3.

Table 7.3 Terms Used in Purchase Order

Payment term	Payment value percentage
Submission of drawing	10
80% material receipts	70
On supervision	15
Commissioning & Testing	5

From the above discussions it can be concluded that the culture of integrated supplier, which is supporting the ERP concept, is found to be absolutely missing.

When we see inventory valuation and accounting point of view, Indian ERP users lack good practices. In one chemical company, most of the spare parts were considered as expensed items or cost items or *non-inventory* items in ERP perspective. The typical problem with such items is then its physical existence versus accounted consumption. The materials head demanded flexibility of accommodating consumption of a cost item in last financial year and availability of the same item in this financial year as free of cost item. In fact, he had expected a separate inventory valuation module, which will function independent of material transactions of receipts and issues.

The major flexibility expected by Indian ERP users can be summarized as "I want to do transactions any way, later on it should get corrected." Hence we find demand of provisional entries, temporary databases, notional requirements, etc. The fundamental principle of ERP is **doing right things right at first time** is not understood and deviations are expected to be regularized. We find many of such cases, ultimately making ERP as unused ornament lying in the bank locker.

Some Typical Indian Cases

We have already discussed typicality in Indian transactions. One of the major culprits in ERP malfunction is the taxation system prevailing in our country. In fact, SAP has to come up with a separate Country India Module called *CIN* (actually to be understood as sin). Baan has localization module to suit legal implications, similarly, J.D. Edwards, etc. have tax module to cater to Indian transactional needs. The tax structure itself is complex and terms used by planners make it more complex.

The author has seen how a switchgear manufacturing company (light electrical engineering) suffered heavy losses because of the whims and fancies of tax authorities. The company used to buy certain goods from different state and normal sequence of calculation of tax incidents was, Basic cost-Excise Tax-Sales Tax-Octroi-Loading/Unloading-Freight. The last two were independent components. The sales tax authorities, however, warned the company to add Excise and Octroi first and then calculate sales tax on the total value. On the other hand, the octroi authorities asked to pay octroi on the total value wherein sales tax is included. This is a typical cyclic loop problem which the organization cannot control. To come out of this crisis, the organization started assuming standard rate of sales tax, added it to excise and determined the basic value of Octroi calculation. Then the calculated octroi (on actual) is added back to the excise duty to determine the base for sales tax. Standard ERP cannot support all these, and hence the company decided to exclude the tax incidents for inventory valuation and lost its real benefit of ERP. Consultants suggested some jugglery to overcome the problem, but the company stuck to its decision.

The concept of ERP recommends some of the best practices of linking single item-single purchase requisition-single buyer-single line of purchase order-single supplier. When any company implements ERP, this practice suggested by ERP is normally taken as *irrelevant* in this country. We have a list of items attached to one

one requisition number (indent number is the industrial parlance), we may have in certain cases more than one purchaser for the same or similar items (especially in the case of spare parts, engineering items, project items, where most of the time the purchaser is also not sure of what exactly he is buying and for what purpose). Also, we have multiple suppliers for one item. (When the author was keen in knowing this one item-multiple supplier phenomenon in India, the project GM of a construction company explained it like: *"We never pay to our suppliers; when he refuses to supply further, we find another person to continue the supply, and hence our list of suppliers for an item goes up. In fact, to find out the outstanding accounts payables, one should only count the number of suppliers dealing with the organization.")*

One glass manufacturing company implemented ERP and the stores manager was demanding multiple lines for one purchase requisition. His views were typically nurtured in legacy system and he was looking at ERP as an *advanced legacy system.* Consultants somehow convinced him to adopt one item-one requisition policy, but the problem cropped up in another module. Stores started using multiple requisitions for different items, especially spares like V-belts, O-rings, hoses, pipes, etc. The purchaser had to select one line for each individual item and hence his PO was becoming as lengthy as 35 to 40 PO lines per order. In one case the author saw him raising 80 lines of PO which when printed, took more than 20 pages. The real problem came when the stores department took the material receipt entries of these items. The items were similar with only a slight difference in the description, also because of the multiple lines; the user was selecting the wrong PO line for a particular item. If once such transaction took place, its effects could be realized only at the time of bill passing. Consultants were insisting on correct entries whereas users were shouting against ERP's incapacity to address such things automatically.

Most of the ERP brands support no incoming material inspection, a practice seen worldwide. ERP persists on inbuilt quality than inspection. In India we hardly find these practices being followed, especially with non-BoM items. To address these requirements, a common idea used is to create a warehouse in ERP as "under inspection" and "rejected" etc. The parameter settings in such warehouses are tuned to restrict any issue transaction from these warehouses except transfer to *accepted* warehouses. In reality, after setting these parameters the user later asks for immediate and urgent materials issue from these warehouses. ERP does not allow such transaction and hence physically the material is issued without entry. The problem aggravates when material is issued in part from inspection stock. The organization keeps separate tracking of these issue notes and later entered whenever time permits. In the whole process a wrong picture of inventory availability is shown in the system.

In a cement manufacturing company, the author came across a special procedure for these transactions, called *issue against zero stock.* When the available stock is zero and new material is under inspection, under emergency stores issues the under inspection stock as *issue against zero stock.* Understanding this concept and the ***efforts*** to formalize that into a procedure was an enlightning experience. The user was so excited that he was asking a separate register in ERP for these items.

Most Indian companies follow the hierarchical organization structure. It basically supports the division of power and authority. Hence typical policies exist, such as one cannot sign PO having cost more than Rs. 50,000, or only a particular department can receive packing materials, and so on. The decision control flows from lower hierarchy to upper, and hence ***approval*** has to be taken to decide on any issue. ERP expects empowered and knowledgeable employees and hence found not fitting to such Indian requirements.

In a big cosmetics manufacturing company, the author had seen automation of illogical requirements regarding the purchase order approval procedure. This was demanded by a very top level person. The company went for an ERP and during the purchase module implementation GM-Materials was asking facilities like: "purchase officer should not be able to release a single PO having cost more than the limit specified to him, I only may approve the same PO. In my absence system should pass the right of approval to X person automatically. If X is also not available, then the system should hold the PO, but in emergency cases, the purchase officer may release PO with temporary approval."

We can observe a *confusion* of authorities and delegations here; moreover, it was expected to be automated by ERP.

In practice, The author has seen that purchase officers are very clever and never land up in a scenario where they cross their monetary limit. They use simple rule, when 5 seems to be bigger then 2+2+1 is smaller than 5, individually. They simply break one PO of higher cost into multiple orders of lower costs coming well below the prescribed limit, but totalling to the same huge cost.

In the same company, the stores department started asking for approval notes along with NOC (No Objection Certificate) procedure from ERP. The scenario was that many departments were using the same item and they were supposed to provide requisition for it. If the item allocated to one department is required by the second department, then it should provide an Approval Note along with an NOC from the first department. Again, for this approval and NOCs, there exists a hierarchical control. We really wonder sometimes how these companies make huge profits with such backward mentality. In fact, this company is regarded as one of the best FMCG companies in India.

Customize It

Quite often, multinational ERP companies have to bow down for this demand of users. Customization is very much necessary in ERP implementation but not in the way the user wants. Users must customize their policies only as per ERP practices. ERP implementation is the opportunity to get aligned with world-class practices, and one should not change those practices to suit current practices. Customization of ERP creates multiple problems like huge costs of customization, threat of becoming obsolete either because new versions of ERP cannot be directly appended or due to the fact that support from vendor may not be available all the time, risk of random bugs due to non-tested coding, etc. Against all these, the most of the time the organization gets benefits of customization in terms of avoiding *change management problems*. This resistance to change can really be interpreted as refusal to the best or world class or scientific practices.

Sometimes, the company demands customization for trivial issues like rephrasing of terminologies. One blue chip pharmaceutical company argued with the ERP vendor on the term *work order* used in his ERP brand. Normally, this term is used in all ERP brands in the context of production order. The GM-Manufacturing argued that there cannot be work order for manufacturing but work request. Ultimately, the ERP vendor afraid and said that they could customize it. In fact, we find in some ERP brands the *glossary management* to support these name-change requirements.

The author has seen one major customization in a compressor manufacturing company. They opted for the ERP, which was the best in manufacturing management. Unfortunately, the company did most of the customization in the same module. The company's scenario was Assemble-to-order and Make-to-order. The measure issue with ERP was the weak engineering module of the ERP. The company's main selling strength was in the unique design of compressor and the support to customers after sales. The rest of the functions including manufacturing were expected to be utilities. The clients did not understand the concept of ERP and its fitness to their company at all. Also, the consultants failed to adopt suitable implementation approach. The consultants were from an IT division of the parent automobile manufacturing company that had the same ERP brand at place (actually *misplaced*). That company never manufactured automobiles properly and is now consulting to another company on ERP. Perhaps it was strategic approach to take revenge against what ERP did to them and spread it across.

The **mass customization** required by the clients was completely fulfilled. The ERP product was changed to the extent that the ERP vendor perhaps might not have been in a position to identify his product. The repercussions were like the following:

- MRP became absolutely useless.
- Direct material planning was done through level planning approach or consumption based planning.
- No link was available between manufacturing planning and purchasing, such a link was also not available back from purchasing to assembly planning.
- On-hand inventory information was always wrong.
- Production orders were manually raised and conveniently closed, thus damaging costing of orders.
- System processing time became enormous while operating through finance module.
- Nearly all the operations and decisions became manual.
- The company cannot load new versions of ERP and even patches; if they still want, they have to pay hefty fees again to customize new versions to suit earlier customized version.

This case could be representative where heavy customization takes place. The common reaction of users is "we were doing better earlier, now we have to do double the work; maintain everything manually and also somehow in ERP. Against that what do we get?"

In the case of the big Indian companies, we find another typical feature. They normally are not happy with implementing one ERP. Hence we find in one MNC pharmaceutical company, exhibition of ERP brands. Initially they had BPCS, then they had opted for J.D. Edwards. After acquiring another company, which was using Mfg/Pro, the score of a number of ERP packages went up. Today, they are thinking of adopting SAP to create more **value**. Ironically the store persons say that their original Cobol based system is still better for some transactions, whereas the production planner finds Excel is the best for all the planning requirements. The company uses another *customized system* for data uploading, migration, testing, etc. to meet the major requirements of smooth data flow across all ERPs. Working in such a company automatically provides promising ERP consultants with all the facilities of ERP training school. It seems that the company has enough money to spend on such luxuries.

Lastly, one more point is to be noted regarding the confusion between *configuration* and *customization*. Each ERP product offers enough flexibility to address the varying needs of different industrial sectors. This flexibility can be called *configuarblity* and is available in the ERP systems. This will help users to plan dissimilar, unlike or even special events of transactions. But the user should not take liberty in changing the *basic theme* of ERP through customization. Most of the time, the user argues that the current practice brings him revenue and is not supported by ERP. The answer for this argument is very simple, and that is, one has to prove the argument on statistical basis. Secondly, if the current bad practice brings revenue to the user, then he may not opt for ERP, and can go for some customized software that will automate his current processes. Organizations must think on what is the need to invest crores of rupees on ERP when they add a few more to customize it and then practice as per the current style only.

Conclusion

Barring a few lucky, we find that in most of the Indian companies ERP failed to provide expected returns on investments. The reasons behind this could be anything but ERP is bad. We have discussed many issues in this chapter with supporting examples and cases why Indian companies are not able to extract value out of ERP. Let us now see what exactly ERP has offered to Indian companies even after it was condemned as "failed".

Understanding of Existing Bad Practices

Every user will agree on this point that ERP *exposed* them. The fundamental approach of BPR, *why do at all what we do*, helped users to understand where exactly they fall short over world-class practices. It has helped them in understanding what is wrong even though they may do it. This is great contribution of ERP.

Integrated Approach

ERP forcefully generates an atmosphere of integrating all the activities in the organization. In fact, this is the reason also why it has been resisted. It has created some level of resource planning through overall organization assimilation. Slowly, it is building a culture of doing things together, decentralized empowerments, quick and information based decisions, skipping non-value adding procedures, and mainly directing all the resources as per specified objectives.

Disciplined Actions

Most organizations now at least understand what is discipline, especially the importance of data entry in time and correctly maintaining appropriate masters, generating proper information to revise master values, identification of exact goal, and allocation of all the resources for it without any later deviation, operating standardization, attitude of doing right things at the first attempt, etc.

Information

Many organizations started knowing about themselves during ERP implementation. It includes information about items, their consumption patterns, typicality in storing and issue, inventory costs, machine performance and productivity figures, number of sales persons on sites, number of instruments lying unused, what HR department consumes, etc. Such ainformation is not generated but required to be set in ERP. Such a demand for setting parameters has prompted to carry out studies as well as make attempts which helped the organization to understand itself better.

Planning Maturity

Ultimately, ERP provides information and not anything beyond that. It is up to the user how he or she utilizes it for the decisions and actions. Most of the Indian planners are still in the MS-Excel age, and not exactly utilizing ERP for planning. But few have realized the powerful approach of ERP to decide on the resource allocations. It helped them in becoming more matured in terms of following scientific and accurate methods, thinking beyond data and looking at data patterns, focusing on most appropriate goals along with polished and comfortable working, using IT. Even though the pace of such learning is very low, it is happening.

Master System

You like it or not, you can't replace it, this is the scenario of ERP in India. Every company, if it has gone for ERP, cannot discount it because of many reasons: cost of investment, no other system is available now to address all that ERP gives, and all masters are now available at one place. ERP masters can be understood as the complete biodata of the company and can serve as the basic reference place for all the decisions including changing old policies to framing new policies. All the advanced systems like SCM, CRM, or even CAD/CAM, etc. have to *talk* with ERP for their performance. ERP thus is imperative.

EXERCISES

1. Explain the current ERP market scenario in India.
2. "Successful ERP implementation in India will primarily depend on selection of consultants." Discuss.
3. What are the various reasons behind ERP failures in India?
4. The major enemy of ERP is the mindset of user. Comment.
5. Discuss the contributions of ERP to Indian industrial sector.

CHAPTER 8

Making ERP "To Be"

In Chapter 7, we have analyzed the present scenario of ERP in Indian companies. In this chapter, we will discuss in detail the methodologies, policies, and the understanding required to make ERP implementation a great success in these companies.

PREREQUISITES OF ERP

We have seen in Chapter 2 that the ERP concept is based on five major business policies. To make ERP implementation fruitful, these are the recommended practices. We can describe now the essential cultural elements based on these practices to make ERP a great success:

- Highly customer focussed environment
- Hierarchy and boundaryless structure with empowered employees
- Well-defined process based activities
- Responsible and accountable process ownerships

The absence of any one of the above will lead to ERP malfunction. Hence to make the successful implementation, ERP must be properly interpreted in the following ways:

- ERP is more a business strategy than IT strategy.
- The concept of ERP is more suitable for the *lean manufacture* than *mass manufacture*. In fact, in assemble to order scenario, ERP brings excellent business results, whereas in *make to order* scenario, it goes beyond business results and improves employee morale and motivation.
- The culture of *make to stock* is not at all suitable to ERP, and hence forceful implementation of ERP will make ERP degenerate into more of a *transactional system* than a planning system, thereby losing its core inherent capability.

- The typical qualities of ERP users include: team spirit, analytical mindset, readiness to be a change agent, willingness to accept process accountability, viewing IT as a tool for scientific experimentations and improve information level.
- The chief issue of ERP is not the process, not the technology but the people. Hence, the Human Resource Head should be the main project leader for the ERP exercise.

From this it will be very clear why exactly some companies in India are not able to implement ERP successfully. First, the Indian companies have to tune their business strategies more towards consumer requirements than customers, thus leaving forecasting at least for the finished goods. The second major issue is the traditional function based allocations of resources and nonexistence of process based set-ups. It is not simple to change everything in a day, but at least there should be a plan for doing it.

Secondly, while selecting ERP users, normally no special exercise is carried out in the organization. It is conveniently assumed as to who was doing whatever job yesterday will be continuing to do the same in the ERP environment. This mentality is very dangerous and also indicates very low level of significance attached to ERP concept in the organization. In fact, when the chief guest or chairman inaugurates annual get-together, the HR manager takes at least five hours to scrutinize who is supposed to offer bouquet at what time, from which direction the chief guest should enter, etc., but when it comes to ERP user selection problem, he *empowers* the immediate superior of user or Functional Head to decide on such non-HR issues. This creates the selection process biased and only based on business performance rather than on the person's behaviour. Such a scenario sometimes includes completely indifferent behaviour of the HR department towards ERP implementation in the company. There are a few reported cases where the HR Head was not even aware of the proper name of the ERP brand, which has been implemented in his company. The typical outlook to ERP is more of computerization or automation project than the effective tool for strategic allocations and improvements in the HR side of the company. The exceptions were found when the ERP implementation was carried out primarily for the HR department.

ERP *PANCHANGA* (FIVE ELEMENTS): MAKING ERP SUCCESS

Let us now discuss which are the critical elements of ERP and what way ERP can be made a success story. Figure 8.1 shows the essential and critical elements of ERP success with their focusing style.

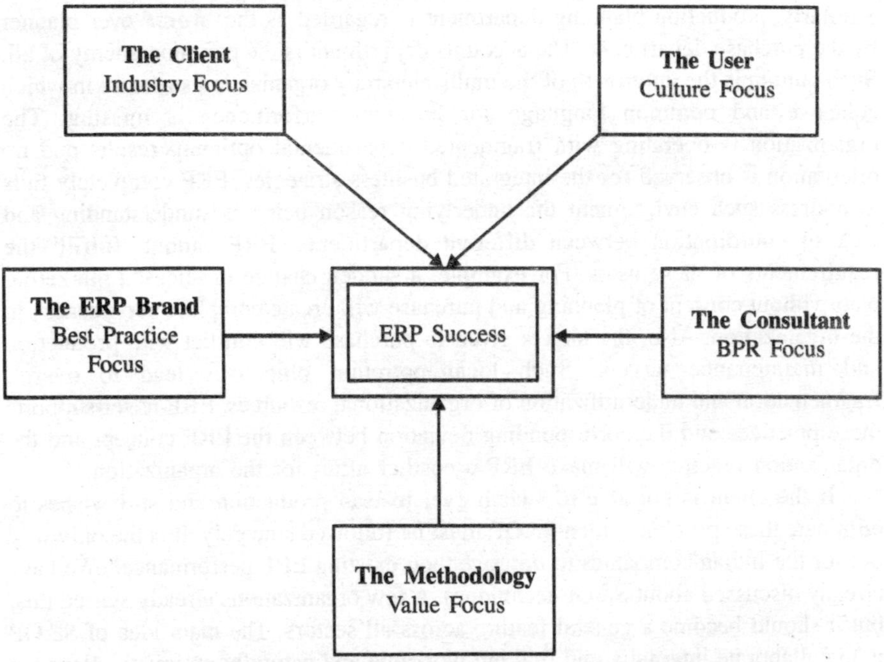

Figure 8.1 Model for ERP success: *Panchanga* (Five elements) of ERP.

To make ERP implementation sensible, we have to consider these five elements along with its focusing styles and then formulate the overall plan of actions. Let us now analyze the every element in detail.

The Client

The first and foremost element is the client, who suggests to focus on the organization's main line of business. As ERP implementation is more of business strategy than IT strategy, one has to analyze the key business drivers specific to the industry and also for the company. It is customary to redefine the business processes with proper synchronization of these drivers along with improved customer interactions. The term *customer* includes internal as well as external. The organization must plan for leaving traditional functional set-ups and reconfiguring its resources across pull type process set-ups where every transaction has specified supplier, customer, and the activities known in all respects.

In most of the Indian companies we find that, even after adopting ERP, the organization continues with traditional functional style of departmentalization. This is mainly because of the absence of customer driven strategic plan or its incomplete implementation. In such set-ups or typically in *make-to-stock* environment, we find the traditional atmosphere of rivalry between various functional departments. For example, Marketing is the main 'culprit' for the production planning inefficiencies because of the *dynamic, non-standard requirements* which do not make sense.

Similarly, production planning department is regarded as the '*worst*' ever planner by the purchase department. The accounts department is the common enemy of all. Such culture is the outgrowth of the multi-hierarchy organization structure in which cohesive and common language for business performance is missing. The organization is operating with fragmented departmental optimum results and no orientation is observed for the integrated business strategies. ERP completely fails to address such environment the underlying reason being misunderstanding and lack of coordination between different departments. ERP cannot 'fulfill' the requirements of these users. For example, a sudden change in released marketing plan without consent of planning and purchase will create complete nervousness in the organization. Also, the targets given to purchase will conflict with production and maintenance targets. Such local optimum objectives lead to overall fragmentation and underutilization of organizational resources. ERP never supports these practices and the corresponding deviation between the ERP concept and the organization practice will make ERP a costlier affair for the organization.

If the client is not able to switch over to lean production and still wishes to eliminate these problems, then S&OP must be followed sincerely. It is the only way out for the Indian companies to improve their existing ERP performance. (We have already discussed about S&OP technique). A few organizations already started this, but it should become a general feature across all sectors. The main idea of S&OP is to collaborate internally and find out workable and naturally optimistic plans for particular planning horizon. Participating regularly in such meetings will boost the morale of participants for driving ERP towards success. An important point to be noted here is that this recommendation is applicable to each and every industrial sector including manufacturing and service.

The User

We have already discussed that the success or failure of ERP implementation greatly depends upon who is using it. We find in India various views of users towards ERP. Most of the time these opinions are based on the organization culture. The word "culture" is used here to connote the average IT acquaintance of the overall users. In India we find normally four different cultural transformations prevailing during ERP implementation:

1. From no system to ERP system
2. From manual systems to ERP system
3. From computerized system to ERP system
4. From ERP system to ERP system.

On an average, at least two scenarios do exist in most of the Indian companies. We find sometimes all the four types exist in one organization itself. The characteristics of the users in all the four cases are different and hence the user element in all scenarios must be managed accordingly.

Surprisingly, most of the ERP users who have retained their jobs after ERP talks, it is a good system for disciplined company than their own, because discipline is not part of their company. Another assessment of ERP by the users is that ERP is a *job killer*, hence attempts are made to kill ERP first. Most of the users of this school of thought found successful in their mission but unsuccessful in retaining their job. ERP has nothing to do with the downsizing, but it may possibly recommend redeployment of people in appropriate areas. We have to agree on certain issues like so many years the organization had built a mentality of not owning responsibility (or 'saving one's skin') in the employees, which immediately cannot be changed within a year or so.

ERP expects boundaryless flat organization structure where every employee is a decision maker and not a mere follower. Secondly, the decision-making must be scientific than based on *gut feel*. Thirdly, ERP assumes that the user has an indepth knowledge of the process he is associated with. He has to work in a team as a key resource element. The objective of the user is to pass maximum value to the customer than to create his own convenience. The user must be analytical in his thinking and be able to use information generated through data iterations for more effective and informed decisions.

To become such a user, one has to get trained and more trained, and later self trained. But most of the ERP training in India is more of software training. The user is shown various screens of the ERP system and taught how to enter what he was doing previously. No trainer ever explains to him why he should enter there, what are the repercussions of his entries in other modules, how to use the best out of multiple settings, why a particular setting is made like that, etc. In fact, the reality that every entry is the financial entry and ultimately gets posted into General Ledger and posted in turn into Profit & Loss Account or Balance Sheet is never realized by the user during training or even after implementation. This feel of responsibility is extremely essential for the user to become a mature ERP user.

One typical problem we see in India is the age of ERP users. In manufacturing industries we find many people are above 40–45 years of age, and are designated as key ERP users. The delicate relationship between their resistances to ERP with the lack of computer knowledge has to be resolved. They should be educated enough to overcome the common computer phobia of *slow learning and fast forgetting*. These users who have seen the company in the past so many years, naturally get offended when consultants younger to them and with less years of experience advise them.

To enhance the interest of users Indian companies must make a point of user training, focusing on ERP and not merely on tools for ERP, i.e. ERP brand, which they have bought. Ideally, the training programme should be designed to cater to individual needs and hence carefully planned.

Secondly, the empowerment has to be planned slowly but positively over a period. This should include removing ridiculous and conflicting targets, thus helping the users to participate in making ERP a success.

The Consultant

The role of consultant is exactly what Krishna did in *Mahabharata* war. He had not taken any weapon in hand but only provided *ideas*. The same is expected in the war of ERP implementation where the user is the *Arjuna*. Unlike Arjuna the user is confused and frustrated every moment. The user has to be motivated, directed, educated and has to take stand for ERP. It is not an exaggeration to say that the first step of ERP adoption should be the selection of consultant and then the rest. Many Indian ERP projects are *As Is* just because of *consulting performance* coupled with the *user performance*. We are referring the term consultant here in the sense of 'Functional Consultant' and not the Technical Consultant whose job is normally not affected by users as such.

Most of the time companies curse consultants for

- poor industry knowledge,
- lack of knowledge on client's key success factors for business,
- lack of understanding user's perspectives,
- lack of consulting experience,
- adamant attitude, and
- no loyalty or interest for solving problems.

It is very sad to state that all the above do exist in reality. One user in an automobile company mentioned that "consultants know nothing; they come here, learn from us and then vanish one day for the self-betterment without solving our problems." Fortunately, consultants are not blamed normally for their poor ERP product knowledge.

In early days of implementation (till 1996), we found anybody having graduation in any discipline with master's degree in computer applications (MCA) was eligible for ERP consulting, especially in technical consulting. The simple economics rule exists of high demand versus short supply. Such people were learning through ERP implementation projects and hence the above arguments against consultants were found justified. Now the scenario is changing. Most of the consultants are professionally qualified along with considerable functional experience.

The prime focus of consultant should be on the reengineering of existing set-ups in the client's side to improve ERP performance. This demands that the ERP consultant must be a good business consultant first. At least he should know who is Michael Hammer and Champy. The expected qualities of the ERP consultant could be enumerated as he

1. must have adequate level of pure functional experience
2. must be thorough with ERP product
3. should have excellent HR skills with unique convincing abilities
4. must be tuned to process improvements than automation
5. should have well-balanced temperament and composed personality.

The critical role normally played by a consultant is to remove various 'orphan' activities and address them in a proper manner. One typical example of this orphan activity was observed in a heavy engineering company. The design department activity was observed in a heavy engineering company. The design department used to claim that making Bill of Materials was their job, but selecting and arranging branded components required by customer should be the purchase level decision. And the problem was, purchase may select some economical brand, which in turn affects the performance of some other assembly, hence again, the design department comes into picture. The process was continuous and creates a lot of back and forth interactions for one decision. Users were demanding the *automation* of such discussions across departments in ERP. Sometimes smart consultant takes this as an opportunity to revamp the whole process of BoM structuring in the organization. He convinces the client to form a cell of BoM structuring for complicated customer configurations. The cell consists of each user from marketing, engineering, planning, production, purchase, and also from accounts. In fact, he had *reengineered* the functional set of the organization into a temporary process set-up for improving decision-making quality and speed.

Such a smart consultant follows a few general guidelines regarding BPR preparations required during consulting:

1. User's psychological understanding of ERP is best defined by his legacy system's understanding.

This rule will help him in convincing the user who says:

> "I want distributed computing and temporary databases in ERP to create more work to avoid chitchatting of people."
>
> "ERP is slower than the manual system; till the time system 'opens' I get information manually, hence my visual manual systems are better."
>
> "I must get multiple prints of the document in various colours like yellow, pink, green and white, because each will go as copy to various departments for actions."
>
> "Give me various types of purchase receipt documents (GRN); one is called clear GRN where PO exists, second is pending GRN where PO doesn't exist, but excise gate pass exists, third is where PO exists but excise gate pass doesn't exist, fourth is ...
>
> "GRN is the final document, hence I write Lorry Number on backside of it. Henceforth let ERP print it on backside automatically."

2. User's demand on security issues in ERP is the threat of peoples' capability.

   This rule may help the consultant to tackle cases where the user insists on restricting the free flow of generated information, wrong master settings, approval hierarchies, material accounting not to be done automatically but through accounts department only, etc.
3. The user's view of flexibility is the deliberate demand for lack of system control to accommodate the so-called transactional convenience.

Hence the consultant can boldly face the scenarios where the user says:

> "I have passed the sales entry, excise entry also; now I want to modify

only sales entry."

"Excisable item is going out; give me facility to put some Cenvat credit of the similar item because I don't know exactly which item is going out and what was its original valuation along with what excise amount I credited against it."

4. The user demands are unrealistic because he doesn't know that the strength of ERP is not matching the full strength of all the IT applications like CAD/CAM, work flow management, optimization, simulating tool, etc.

The consultants can successfully convince the user who demands:

"I want to run MRP selectively, but the recommendations should be applied to all items with certain exceptions specified by me; hey, give me interactive MRP."

"Why not ERP pick up drawing, allow me to edit only the title and revision number in it, further checks who is available on that day and then automatically warns the engineer for release note, then the control should move to ..."

"I want to see the simulation first and then I will select the course of action."

"Give me the Pie chart, Normal curve and also to determine service level ERP should give me graphical selector and interactive sessions."

5. "Give me policy, I will give you practice."

Most of the time, the user is not in a position to analyze what way he should address his processes for value creation. It is the job of consultants now to take only the policy decisions from users on various scenarios and then design, map and implement the process suitable to user's culture. In such cases, it is better to avoid discussions and further discussions. For example, in one chemical company, the same item was available in domestic as well as in imported market. The price difference was more than 250%. Since the company follows standard costing, ideally there should be different identification for the same item having such price differences to account for inventory costs separately because it has not implemented Lot Control Module. The client was unable to understand the need of separate code of the item, and the poor consultants were not able to convince the accounting repercussions to hardcore functional guy from stores. Since the user doesn't understand commercial, operational and legal implications of the process completely in the ERP, consultants should exhibit dominating role in such cases to ultimately give the best out of ERP to the user.

6. Most of the questions of the users can be answered by the following arguments:

Because system is on-line

Because system is integrated across organization

Yes, possible through proper configuration of parameter settings

That value comes from master setting

The consultant who can manage the implementation with the above qualities and techniques can turn around the whole scenario of Indian ERP into new version of successful enthusiasm.

The Methodology

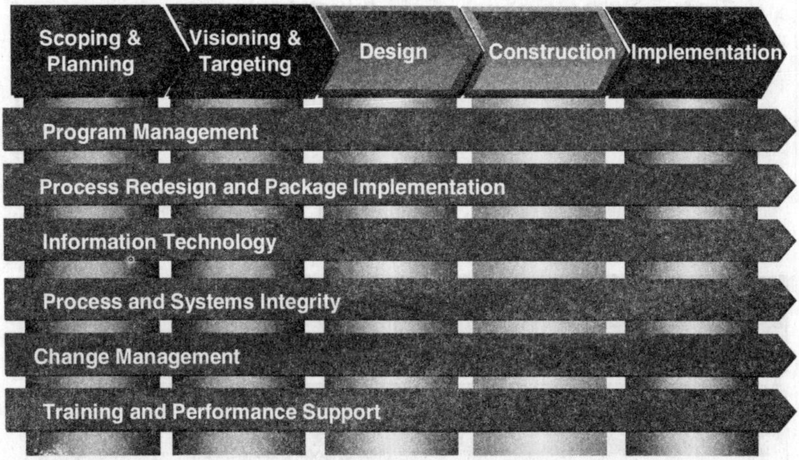

Figure 8.2 Express Methodology.

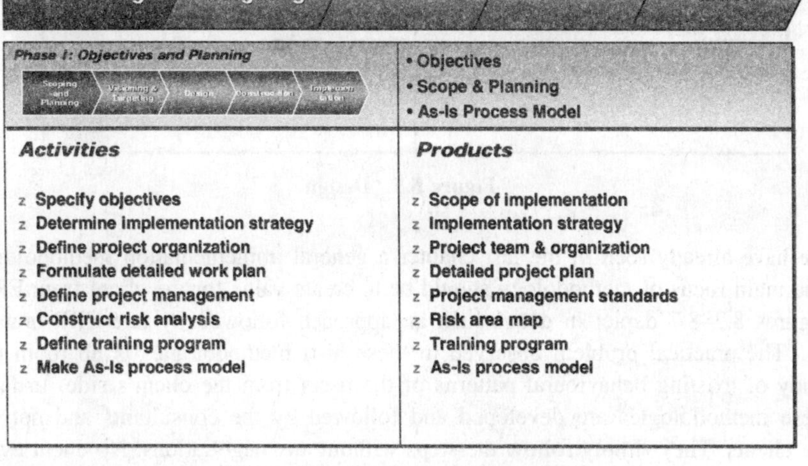

Figure 8.3 Scoping and Planning.

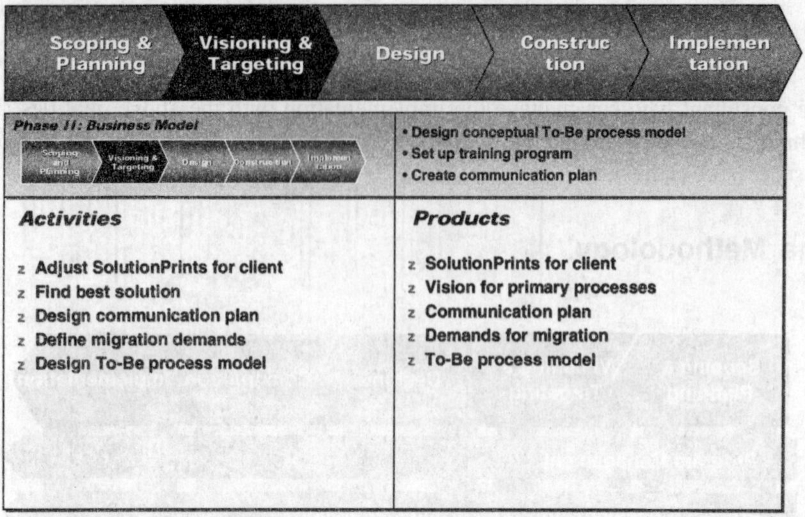

Figure 8.4 Visioning and Targeting.

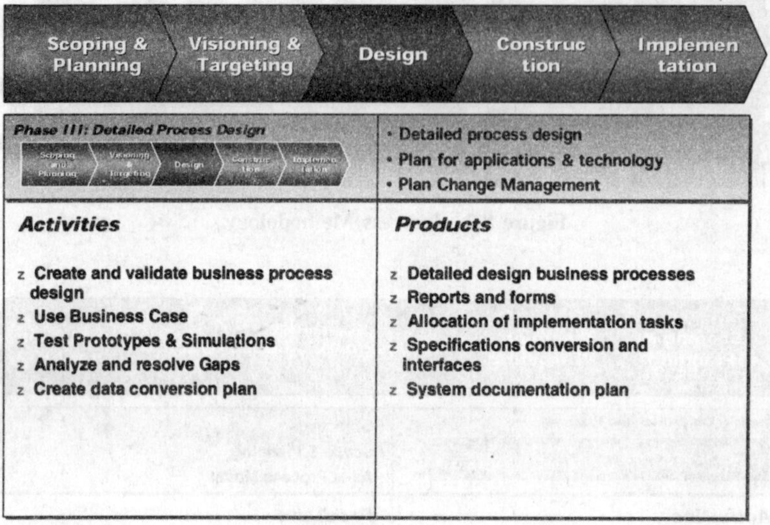

Figure 8.5 Design

We have already seen in the last chapter a general implementation methodology. The main focus of methodology should be to create value for the client from ERP. Figures 8.2–8.7 depict in detail such an approach followed by one ERP brand.

The practical problem observed in these hi-fi methodologies is no room for study of existing behavioural patterns of the users from the client's side. In fact, these methodologies are developed and followed by the consultants and not by the clients. They simply follow the steps without any negotiations. No client even thinks of some input plan to consultants regarding the specificity of the organization. Hence we find no interactive elements in the methodology.

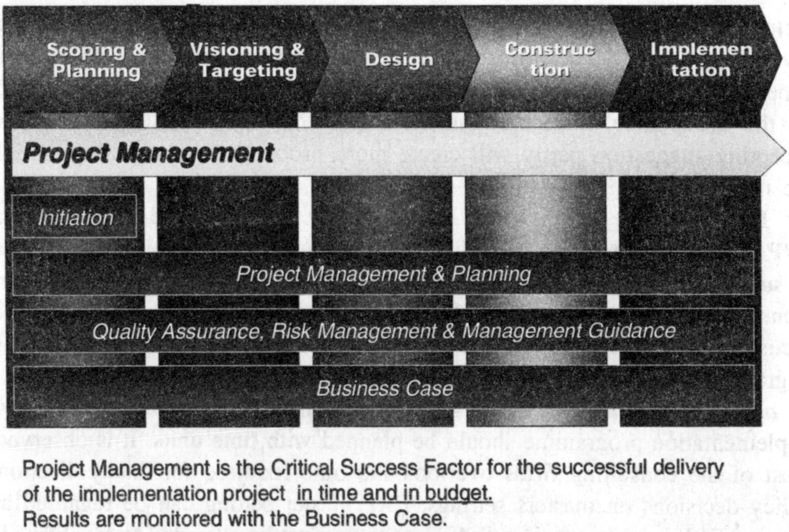

Figure 8.6 Construction

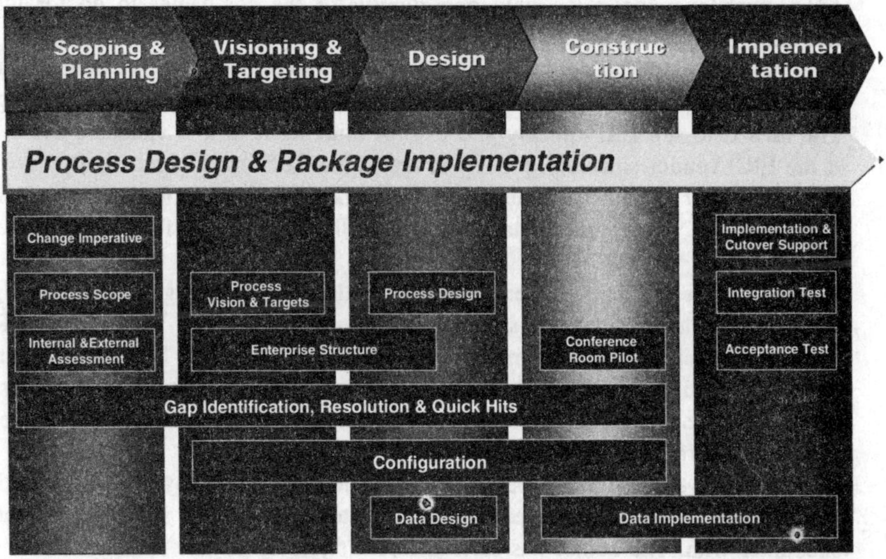

Figure 8.7 Implementation

As we have already discussed, the user characteristics are developed over a period of time and governed by a member of parameters. The success of the ERP is directly based on the reconfiguration of standard ERP implementation methodology based on user' characteristics. Secondly, most of the time in India the spelled methodology remains in the document and actually something different happens. These major issues are required to be sorted out for ERP success.

A good methodology starts from the preliminary analysis of ERP readiness audit for the client. This itself is a subject for a separate book; hence we take recourse by discussing only the key issue concerning it. The analysis should include the current business performance of the client, forthcoming strategic plans, investment potentials, culture and general human resource characteristics, expectations, and objective settings for ERP. The client has to take major decision on the acceptance of recommendations provided by the study. As we know, accepting suggestion partly will create more problems than rejecting completely the implementation programme.

Looking at the current trend, it may be very risky from the client side to reject ERP based on poor readiness audit results. To sustain competitiveness ERP cannot be substituted by fragmented legacy systems. Hence the only way out is the proper reengineering programme for ERP adoption. This should be the critical and main focus of the methodology. The business **blue print** should not only talk of migration and other things but also discuss more on the scientific analysis of *to be adoption* and its phasewise executions. Then the activities for the overall implementation programme should be planned with time units. It is observed that most of the consulting firms overlook the time required for data collection and policy decisions on masters settings. ERP master setting can be regarded as the heart of ERP implementation. Sufficient time must be allocated to identify, clarify, validate and simulate the exact information about all the master level entries. In India, such exercise is the only opportunity for the companies to do for their lifetime better performance. It will not be false if we say that an organization of size more than 1000 crores should take at least three months to set Item Master. No consulting company or the client will agree on such figures in today's jet age. The idea is to sell ERP quickly and to start utilizing it. It is a vicious cycle that, if the ERP vendor sincerely quotes the real figures of time budget, surely he will lose the order because of the clients tendency to bargain foolishly on such parameters. A golden mean has to be skilfully worked out for proper project execution and success.

One more critical element is the parallel user training and knowledge upgrading. Ideally, the consultant should take users to the actual ERP implemented sites to show them the process flow. What you see is the best training you never thought of, especially when you have no idea or clue for such concepts (Of course, the consultant should have sufficient courage to make such visits where his past performance is known).

The *go live* phase has to be properly planned and under any circumstance the organization should be equipped with abilities to face whatever shortcomings they encounter with. The author has seen different styles of go live strategy in one of the jewelry manufacturing companies. The consultant recommended ten transactions every day to be carried out in ERP without any entry in legacy system. Then he used to generate all the documents from ERP as supporting papers for the manual entries and reports. The rest of the entries in a day used to be carried as manual entries in the legacy system. Soon users understood ERP is better on all the grounds. His formula worked wonderfully well for generating confidence and reduction in resistance in users' mind. Perhaps, this was workable because of the small size of the organization. But such innovative ideas must be planned and used in developing implementation methodologies. We find many ideas of implementation roll outs when the organization goes for a multisite project.

Another question is, should we implement ERP module wise or all the modules at one go? The answers to these questions are case specific. We cannot *generalize* the theory for it: The decision drivers could be readiness audit results, available strength of consulting human power—both internal and external—relevance of ERP at various sites, timeframe, and the budget. But we can generally recommend that ideally, the organization should go for the implementation of all the modules at one site, and then go for roll out strategy for all sites.

The implementation methodology should also suggest the framework for the post-ERP implementation audit and further optimization. It should clearly define metrics for success measurement. These measurements should be based on statistical design and should be realistic. Normally, some thumb rules are applied to gauge ERP performance, but that is not the right method.

Lastly, let us discuss on a very interesting question of chicken-egg paradox associated with ERP implementation. The organization should first carry out BPR and then implement ERP, or vice versa. Actually, one has to understand that the physical form of the BPR concept is the ERP system. The author has seen four cases where BPR is carried out first and then ERP was implemented. All these places, the BPR document was thrown into dustbin and new *To Be document* was prepared suitable to ERP. Needless to say that for both the projects, different consultants were engaged. The organization had invested approximately Rs. 6.5 million (on average) in BPR and about Rs. 20 million in ERP. These cases clearly show that BPR benefits as such don't exist without ERP reference, and ERP just cannot be carried out without proper BPR. From the client's side, we have to assume that BPR must be the outgrowth of ERP implementation and, therefore, it should be carried out during implementation only. But the major element of BPR is the change in the mindset, which can be initiated before ERP adoption, may be during preliminary analysis by way of user training. The role of consultant in this case is to carry *noiseless BPR* which triggers the implementation smoothly. This typically includes the set of tricky techniques of changing organization's processes along with user mindset without any formal declaration of BPR. It avoids conflicts and enable to face resistance.

The ERP Brand

How to select the ERP brand perhaps became difficult today was not the case a few years back. Most of the time budget was the main criteria for elimination round and then companies used to see the live customer list of ERP vendor. We can very well say that the ERP buying decision is like any other procurement decision. For example, when a buyer purchases bearing, normally he analyzes quality, cost, service and response time to choose the particular vendor. All these parameters were applied in ERP buying also. In fact, a few ERP vendors have come up with industry specific solutions, which, in the true sense, is more of a marketing strategy than an operations specificity.

Secondly, because of the very competitive environment and market saturation, ERP vendors have decreased their prices and hence the SME segment is also aspiring for such world-class solutions. We also find a trend of *in-house development* of ERP. Such companies are also now found significant in numbers in India.

While selecting the ERP brand, the focus should be the availability of the best practices or the world-class practices in the software. If we examine closely, we find various ERP products are strong in various functional modules. This strength could be in terms of availability of various planning options, tight control on orphan processes, excellent functional flow, easy and user-friendly reporting, graphical presentations, automatic routing through world-class valued added processes. The problem is how to know which ERP is strong where and how that will synergize the client's business results. To solve the first question, to some extent, we can refer literature in the form of reports and articles. The commercial presentation of the ERP vendor and later discussions may help further. The main question is which strength one should look for. This problem has to be handled with a detailed case study of the organization. From the strategic point of view, the organization has to understand the vital processes for the revenue impact as well as the bottomline. Thus efforts should be directed to find the thrust area with proper reasoning. Accordingly, one can match the requirements with the strengths of ERP to proceed further. It is also observed that some clients go for multiple ERP products to get equipped with all the strengths available of all the products. Such decisions have to be validated on the basis of training costs, middleware software and processes cost, and loss of real integration in financial accounting grounds. We see such multi-ERP enabled companies not being able to use those strengths. In fact this approach of adopting multi-ERP is not at all required in our country on the cost-benefit criteria. An organization which is already very stable in implementation of one ERP may think of such option, but in that case also, the preferable alternative is to improve the existing ERP rather than adopting new. Multi-ERP adoption leads to countless problems which may crop up due to data loading, automatic migration, linking with various functionality, user understanding, effective parameter settings, redundancy and violations, etc. Moreover, many a time, ERP vendors cannot be helpful on service problems if multiple ERP products are involved. In case some other company has been merged into the parent company or in such similar instances, where both companies have different ERP, then the problem of system uniformity has to be resolved either by scraping one system or keeping separate installations and then capturing only financial implications in the main system to evaluate overall effects. In any case, no strict guideline could be developed, as most of the issues are people specific and less technology specific. In this context, the good news is that though we find functional dominance of certain functionality in various ERP products, more or less they are all similar in the other areas. Therefore, sticking to one ERP brand is always advisable.

Ideally, the organization should go for branded solution of reputed vendor who has at least a few installations in India, preferably in a similar industry. Another issue to be considered is the consulting and support service available for the ERP product. The company should take a prudent decision on these concerns. We have already discussed the consulting requirements.

The next point to be discussed is whether the client should go for individual modules of ERP instead of the full suit of ERP. Barring a few exceptions we find a good trend that no standard ERP product is available in such *modular pack size.* What they recommend is to implement whichever modules are required, but the product will contain full suit and there won't be any price negotiation on this. The main point is the erroneous request from the client side to demand only certain modules. ERP as a concept cannot support these views. The author has seen a few companies where only finance module is implemented. Frankly speaking, ERP in such cases used to be costlier and sophisticated *tally system.* Similarly, we find demand only for distribution or manufacturing system, which is nothing but either a DRP or MRP-II systems with ERP flavour. Such decisions will never help the organization in the long run.

Finally, we will discuss the fate of *in-house* ERP development programme. One has to understand that development of ERP is not like other software development projects, which are normally carried out focusing on automation. We find such serious mistakes being committed by a few giant and many small companies in India. The EDP department in most of the cases is responsible for such in-house development work. They do consult with outside consultants, but the basic **theme** of ERP is completely found missing in these types of products. Standard ERP product development used to cost billions of dollars on research, testing and development investments listing more than ten years. This has been the experience of world-class processes, people, and also the technology. Looking at the present Indian efforts and approaches, it is very difficult to believe that the EDP department will come up with such international standard ERP product. We are not saying that it won't happen, but its not even advisable today to do all these. When we talk of **core-competency**, we should leverage where we have strengths and, instead of building up new strengths, coopt a partner for the missing strengths. Today, when standard ERP products are well within the reach of most of the companies, we should not opt for costly in-house development. This ERP is not at all ERP except integration. The essence of ERP is the free BPR, which is absolutely not happening with these products. If we describe this in-house development correctly, then we can say that such approach is typically observed in software Development Company where only the *specification gathering and automation* takes place.

We see some industrial sectors in India such as power, project or construction where these trends are much more visible. These companies argue that their requirements are different and unique, and no standard ERP could handle efficiently. The second argument is not very correct because we find famous ERP brands have already come up with utility, project, and construction specific solutions also. The first argument is valid that the requirements of these sectors are unique and different. Because we won't really find elsewhere such ineffective control measures that prevail in construction, project and especially power sector in India. May be this is because of *license Raj,* old and traditional set-ups, monopoly type market, absence of professional approach, and rough life styles. The requirement of these sectors is mainly to address the existing processes than providing well-mapped processes. Typically, such requirement was spelled out by the GM-Projects from one construction company that "I should be able to pass entries for the last financial year even after closing of the books by reopening it." Forget equipping this, one really wonders how people think *uniquely* and *differently*.

Embracing standard ERP is the lifetime opportunity for Indian companies to revamp and streamline their existing performances to the level of best practices. One should not miss such an event by making extreme mistakes of in-house development or by adopting multi-ERPs or, accepting only few modules of ERP.

Conclusion

Today in India, in a real sense we fight with ERP regarding its capabilities of addressing of the transactional procedures, rather than its planning logic and mechanisms, which would be needed to be understood, analyzed, and perhaps challenged to extract more value from ERP.

The overall performance of the five key success factors for ERP as depicted in Figure 8.1 must be managed to ensure the successful journey of ERP implementation.

We can correlate one example to ERP status in India. Anybody who wishes to buy a new vehicle can select two normal options. He or she can enroll in the driving school, get trained and then buy the vehicle, and use it. The other option could be to buy the vehicle first and then learn on it by taking risk of accidents. In fact, in the earlier option also, no training school can provide you the training on *actual performance,* because most of the time gear and brake controls are with trainer only. Hence when you buy a vehicle after receiving training again, there exists a risk of accidents.

ERP calamity in India is of the same type. Even if you get good package or consulting or not get it, you cannot avoid mishaps. But as practice makes it more perfect, we will definitely learn in the coming years how to drive ERP without accidents and with comforts.

EXERCISES

1. Explain various pre-requisites of ERP.
2. Discuss ERP Panchanga concept.
3. "Poor consulting input leads to poor ERP performance." Do you agree? Give reasons.
4. What are the risk factors in in-house ERP development project?
5. Develop the complete of metrics that can measure ERP performance ir totality.

Bibliography

BOOKS

Arnold, Tony, J.R., *Introduction to Materials Management*, Prentice Hall, Englewood Cliff, New Jersey, 1991.

Bauer, A., Bowden, R., Browne, J., Duggon, J., and Lyons, G., *Shop Floor Control Systems*, Chapman & Hall, London, 1991.

Buck-Emden Rudiger, Galimow, J., *SAP R/3 System: A Client/Server Technology*, Addison Wesley, California, 1996.

Crum Jim, *Using Oracle Applications*, McGraw-Hill/Osborne, BOSS Corporation, California, 2002.

Dobler, Donald, W. and Burt, David. N., *Purchasing and Supply Management: Text and Cases*, 6th ed., Tata McGraw-Hill, New Delhi, 1999.

Edwards J., Miller Joseph, Allen Jacot, and John Stern, *One World: The Complete Reference*, McGraw-Hill, New York, 2001.

Foster Susan, *Oracle E-business Suit 11-I*, 1, John Wiley & Sons, New York, 2001.

Leon Alexis, *ERP Demystified*, Tata McGraw-Hill, New Delhi, 2002.

Mabberley, Julie, *Activity Based Costing in Financial Institutions*, Pitman Publishing, London, 1998.

Martinich, J., *Production and Operations Management*, John Wiley & Sons, New York, 1997.

Plossl, George, *Orlicky's Material Requirements Planning*, McGraw-Hill, New York, 1995.

Sheikh Khalid, *Manufacturing Resource Planning (MRP II) with Introduction to ERP, SCM and CRM*, Tata McGraw-Hill, New Delhi, 2001.

Vollman Thomas, E., Berry W., and C. Whybark, *Manufacturing Planning and Control Systems*, McGraw-Hill, New York, 1997.

ARTICLES

Gupta Shashank, C-procurement: Delivering on the Promised Land in procurement www.wipro.com/insights/B2Bmarketplace.htm

Sourav Kumar, E-procurement: An opportunity for improving profits, http://infoweek.bitpipe.com

E-forceglobal, From Purchasing to Collaborative Commerce, http://www.eforceglobal.com/pdf/whitepapers/eF.WP-eProcurement_10-28-02.pdf

Altekar Rahul, Managing the supply chain by way of supplier partnership, http://www.pslcbi.com/iimm.pdf

INTERNET LINKS

- www.ramco.com/images/pdf/erp/ Ramco_ERP_solution_for_Breweries.pdf
- http://help.sap.com
- www.navision.com
- www.pwc.com
- www.dtic.mil/comptroller
- www.armstronglaing.com
- www.oracle.com
- www.acornsys.com/value
- www.abcforum.com
- www.defenselink.mil/c3i/bpr/bprcd
- www.sbaer.uca.edu/Research/2002/dsi/papers/138.pdf
- www.doors.ch/DOCS/3COM/50068901.pdf
- www.aim.fsu.edu/administration/plans/Phase%20I%20Architeture%20Flowchart%20-%20FAMU.pdf
- www.link2hr.com/WhitePaper.pdf
- www.ibm.com/servers/eserver/zseries/library/whitepapers/pdf/gf225154.pdf
- www.erpweb.com/shared/process/help.htm
- www.abw.com
- www.micromfgsys.com/solutions/vol1
- www.sap.com
- www.ittoolbox.com
- www.gartner.com
- www.idc.com
- www.qad.com

- www.erpevaluation.com
- www.peoplesoft.com
- www.ciol.com
- www.jdedwards.com
- http://www.express_computer.com
- www.baan.com
- www.indiainfoline.com
- www.technologyevaluation.com

Index